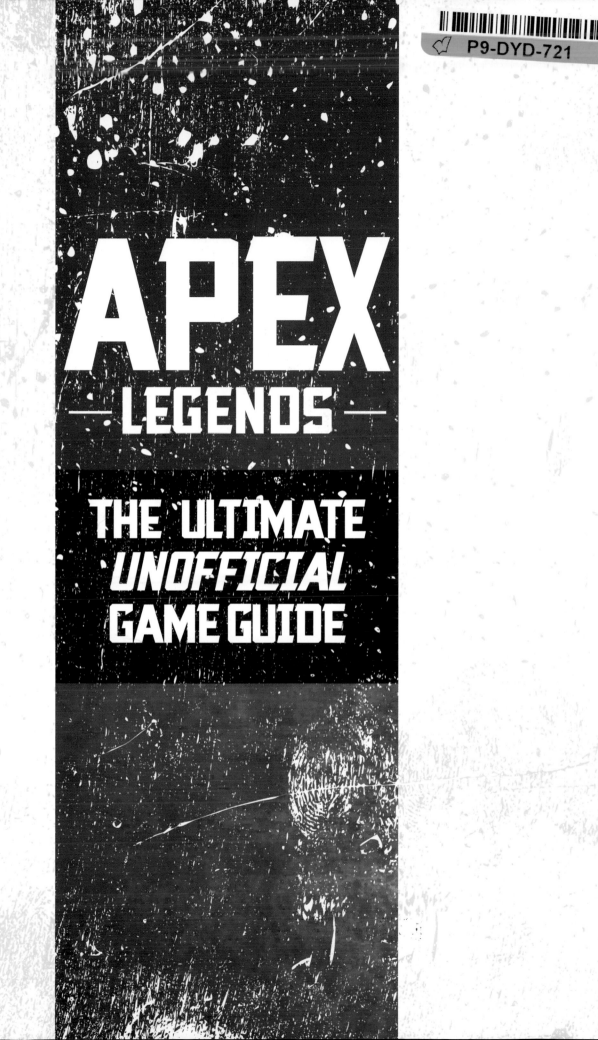

APEX
LEGENDS

THE ULTIMATE *UNOFFICIAL* GAME GUIDE

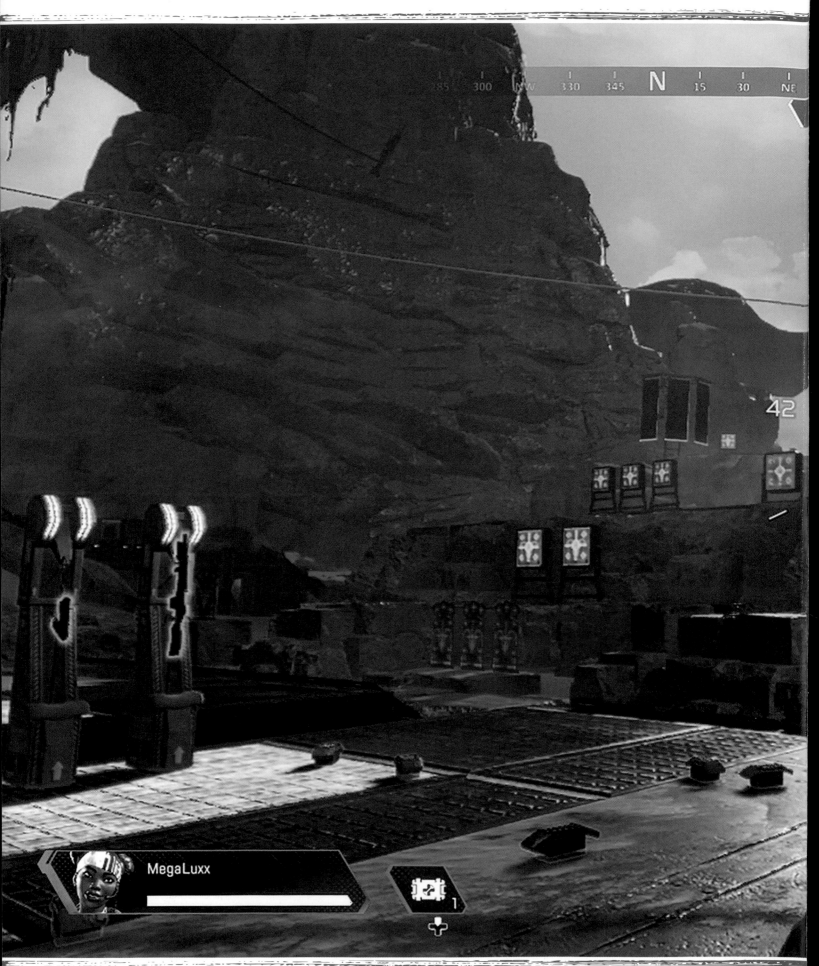

MegaLuxx

This book is available in quantity at special discounts for your group or organization.
For further information, contact:

Triumph Books LLC
814 North Franklin Street
Chicago, Illinois 60610
Phone: (312) 337-0747
www.triumphbooks.com

Printed in U.S.A.
ISBN: 978-1-62937-762-9

Content packaged by Mojo Media, Inc.
Joe Funk: Editor
Jason Hinman: Creative Director

CONTENTS

INTRODUCTION

Apex Legends has quickly become a must-play game. With countless customizations and multiple map options, it opens up fashionable and frenetic new worlds for gamers to enjoy. Plus, it is also regarded as a great "free to play" game for new players to try out.

Mainly character-driven, this game encourages players to customize and take part in who their characters are, what they can do, and how they look. This puts the player in firm control and ensures that their Legend is someone that comes with a name and a background.

As a squad-based game, you're put into the map with others who are working with you in a battle to the death. You're dropped from the sky onto one of many of the places on the map, and will quickly realize that you need to find weapons once you land if you're going to make it.

Your team must work together in order to survive. If they don't, they will soon find that this is the difference between victory and defeat. The team you work with is the team that provides a lifeline, a support system, and the ability to move to the top – together.

Apex Legends is not a typical third-person game where you have to keep moving and dodge incoming fire to win. You need skill and attention to detail to make it out on top, which is more than many of the current crop of games demand.

As a battle game, you do have to duel to the death, but making it to the top requires more finesse and stamina than simply taking out your opponents. While your team works with you to reach the top tiers, you'll develop new skills and battle techniques you didn't know your character had!

6

6

6

6

Bringing something new to the playing field, Electronic Arts has clearly taken the time to listen to players that want a challenging third-person game, and have seemingly managed to provide healthy doses of customization, skill, story, and emotion all in one neatly wrapped package.

You'll soon realize that while this game mimics Fortnite in some respects, this game comes with many differences and certainly much more customization and flexibility.

In the first glimpse of a war-torn environment, players must quickly assimilate to their surroundings and seek out weapons, provisions, and a strategy for survival. Finding and connecting with teammates is key, as collectively you all must operate together if you are going to climb to the top of the game's ranking and bring all those that oppose you, down.

Apex Legends is available on many platforms including PC, Xbox One, PS4, and mobile.

You'll need to have the following minimum specs in order to play on your PC:

- 64-bit Windows 7 operating system

- Intel Core i3-6300 3.8GHz or AMD FX-4350 4.2 GHz Quad-Core Processor

- 6 GB of RAM

- 1 GB or higher GPU RAM and NVIDIA GeForce GT 640 or Radeon HD 7700 GPU

- 30 GB of free space on your hard drive

Legendary competitors are competing against one another, and if you're not legendary then you may want to keep playing, as that is the only way you're going to reach the upper echelons of this game. Begin your quest now for glory, fame, and fortune in this story-based game that provides much more than a free-for-all blaster.

Choose your Legend, strive for glory, and take part in one of the hottest games of the year!

APEX
—LEGENDS—

THE ULTIMATE *UNOFFICIAL* GAME GUIDE

GETTING STARTED

Apex Legends is not a game you can just load-up and start blasting away on. You have to first take the time to choose, create, and make a Legend from the options that the game gives you.

Kickstart your time in the game using our quick start guide and dominate the arena as soon as you're dropped in. It is up to you and your team to work together, use all of the skills your Legends come with, and ensure that you survive the war that awaits.

When you enter into the game, you're greeted with awesome pictures, and an exciting sense of responsibility – will you help your squad make it out on top?

You have to choose your Legend, visit the Armory to equip them, and choose a Battle Pass if you want to sign up for that and use the items and extras that come with it.

The store comes with many extras that you can add to your character, because you can continue to build on them if you choose or you can leave them with the original outfits, weapons, and extras.

8

A BIT OF BACKGROUND ON APEX

The game is set in the Titanfall universe, which is an entire map that is dedicated to the game complete with different cities and terrains to explore. It is a battle royale game, where players are placed in the map and must battle with their teams to the death. The entire team has to be taken out in order to stop the round for the team. Healers can bring back other team members, giving every team a chance to recover.

The setting is around 30 or so years after the events that took place in the game Titanfall 2, where there is a devastating blow that hit the planet from the outer reaches of the solar system. This changed the world as we know it, causing mass destruction.

There is a brief training period that newcomers have to go through, but don't worry, this is all useful information and well worth the time you put in to learn the map and the moves you need to know.

Many players think that they can just jump right in and it works the same way that PUBG and Fortnite work, and while the idea of the map and the battle is somewhat the same, playing is much different, so going through the training is extra important. Trust us, it is worth the little bit extra time to go through training.

Apex Legends has new twists and turns around every corner that most battle royale players may not be expecting when they decide to take the next step.

CHOOSING A LEGEND THAT MATCHES YOUR PLAY STYLE

The Legends come evenly matched with one another when they land in the arena in terms of speed, strength, and firepower but there are also some key traits that set them apart—their abilities. This means choosing the Legend that matches the play style that you perhaps are best at, or prefer playing, can definitely help you, and your team, excel in the game.

With many playing styles such as human shields, confrontational and tough, healing, surprise attacks and more; there is plenty to choose from as you decide if you want to have a more passive or more aggressive Legend based on your own personal playing style.

Of course, if you're unsure of which style you prefer or are the best at then you can try them all out during different matches to find out which you feel the most comfortable playing. The one you get the furthest with might just be the best one to use.

Remember, there are eight different Legends to choose from and which one(s) you decide to invest the time in developing is completely up to you.

Each player has their own finishing move!

This is much different from the other battle royale games that you come across. You can actually perform your own special finishing move on opponents that you're fighting.

The finishing move you get depends on the specific character that you have.

You can even customize your finishing move by finding and using loot boxes in the game, which truly enables you to make your character all your own.

This essentially allows characters to defeat opponents with a bit more pizazz than they'd usually beat them with if they were just running and gunning – which is usually the required norm in just about every other major battle royale game.

IT'S STILL A BATTLE ROYALE GAME

Since Apex Legends it still, ultimately, a battle royale game, the rules and general play are pretty much the same that you'd find with any of the other games of its kind.

This means you have to know where you are at all times as you try to survive inside the shrinking ring of doom. When you enter the circle, it is best to stay away from those highly populated areas where other players spawn, as this is going to bring a high level of combat as soon as you land. If you don't have anything to fight with in hand (and you won't at the start) then you're likely not going to make it.

Any areas at the edge of the circle zone, large cities, or an area that is right under the ship's path will likely have groups of people that landed there at the start of the game.

Smart positioning is crucial to your survival in this game.

USING SMART COMMS

There is an in-game system that can be used to communicate with and ping teammates. You can swap items through this system and even see where they are located on the map if you're not right next to each other.

If you have a microphone plugged in, you can speak with them and let them know where you are, what you have, and where you want to go next. This can be a great advantage that you and your teammates have if you can quickly and efficiently communicate and coordinate actions with voice.

Comms are built into the game, but only keep teammates in touch when paired up so no one else can hear you and your group chat during game play.

STAYING WITH YOUR SQUAD

Since you're split into groups of three, it is essential that you stay with your group. While you are not automatically going to die even if both of your teammates do, it is easier to become the victor if all or most of you are still alive at the end.

Being able to work together as a team is one of the highlights of the game and can also be one of the downfalls if you're not team friendly.

One of the biggest rewards of Apex Legends is the ability to win (and win big) if you are able to keep the squad together and keep them moving. By working together, everyone complements each other while progressing through ever more difficult challenges.

Since everyone in the squad has a different talent, this is going to make overcoming other groups easier if you work together. The right mix of teammates can even be undefeated in a round!

Those that try to go at it as lone wolves only find themselves up against teams that overpower and defeat them. It is not recommended.

KNOW THE ARENA

The map where the matches take place is known as Kings Canyon.

This playground is one that has many different places to explore, nooks and crannies that perhaps have not seen the light of day for some time, and even some cool nuclear fallout bunkers and abandoned military items sprinkled about.

Many different places provide cover in the shape of abandoned buildings as you assess your location and come up with a plan and use the area wisely to overcome your opponents. Some of the vegetation in the area has become so overgrown that you may not be able to see over it.

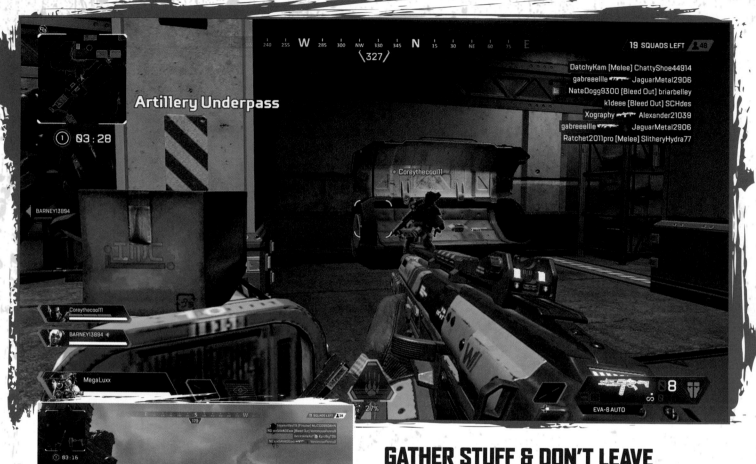

GATHER STUFF & DON'T LEAVE ANYTHING TO WASTE

You may feel a bit like a hoarder, but remember, everything has a purpose in Apex.

One of the biggest, and perhaps among the best, features of this game as compared to others, is that when you pick up a weapon or piece of armor, your inventory will automatically tell you if this is better than what you're currently using. This way, you don't have to bother comparing and contrasting, you can simply switch out to the more superior item.

You should always keep an eye out for great loot and call it out to your teammates. Keeping them well armed, armored, and ready for battle is a must because you're all in this together.

By understanding the map and familiarizing yourself with optimal locations, you can not only help your teammates find the best places to hide and create a camp, but also where the juiciest loot may be hidden. Secret places do exist in Apex, you just have to know where to look.

By knowing the map and your surroundings every time you drop, you're better able to make faster, more calculated decisions and move around more effectively.

There are some specific locations that have higher-end loot throughout the map, and these are known as hot zones. The best stuff, however, come from the drop ships that fall throughout the matches in random places.

You will see these large metal beasts coming from the sky. You will want to get your hands on this loot at least once during your time playing Apex. They have just about everything you can imagine inside them, and include some of the best and even rarest loot items found in Apex.

Just remember, you start the match with no armor or weapons to protect yourself with. It is up to you and your squad to determine if this high-end loot is worth the battle to obtain it. You will also have two types of healing items, one that can be used for your character and one for the armor that you are wearing.

There will be season passes, extra items and skins, as well as rare items EA is going to introduce to the players and in the game. Stay tuned to all they have planned.

Stay sharp during game play, keep your eyes and ears open, while relying on your teammates to do the same. Victory only comes to those prepared. Are you and your teammates ready to take on the title of victor?

CHOOSING A LEGEND

Choosing a Legend is almost as important as staying alive in Apex Legends. Knowing the options to choose from and what to expect from each Legend is going to have a huge impact on your game—and your performance.

One feature that makes Apex stand out from other battle royale games is that you can choose the character you want at the start of each round. You don't have to stick with just one, and the game doesn't automatically, randomly choose a character for you when you begin.

Each of the Legends fills a specific need for a team. Choosing one that you feel comfortable playing is a good way to start, because the game will fill in the gaps by pairing you with complementary characters.

Here are each of the nine characters and classes available for players at the start. We've identified which ones you have to purchase, as only six are free for everyone to play in the beginning.

MEET & GREET WITH THE LEGENDS

Each of the different Legends come with their own unique characteristics and skills. They all have a job in the battle arena and you should select a character you are most comfortable playing.

Learning some backstory on each of them provides a bit of insight as to why they are the way they are, and what they are capable of doing in battle.

BANGALORE

Anita Williams is a 35-year-old professional soldier born into a military family. Her, her parents, and her four brothers all served in the military where she learned tactical combat skills. She is among the best at providing defense, while still maintaining her offense.

She fights in the matches to raise money to travel back to her home base where the remainder of her family lives. She taps her extensive combat and weaponry knowledge to help her and her teammates make it to the top ranks.

- **Tactical Ability: Smoke Launcher**
- **Passive Ability: Double Time**
- **Ultimate Ability: Rolling Thunder**

BLOODHOUND

As a skilled hunter, which is how he got his name, Bloodhound's real name, age, and background is unknown. The mystery of this character is what attracts a lot of people and speculation. The rumors about him range from saying he's either extremely wealthy, a murderer with a secret, a whisperer to the dead, or even a former slave escaped and still running.

As a skilled and knowledgeable tracker of the hunt, Bloodhound's skills are endlessly useful for a top team in a game like Apex.

- **Tactical Ability: Eye of the Allfather**
- **Passive Ability: Tracker**
- **Ultimate Ability: Beast of the Hunt**

CAUSTIC – PURCHASE

Known to all as the toxic trapper, his name is Alexander Nox and he runs gruesome experiments using different gases. As one of the brightest minds in the lab where he works, he is constantly trying to develop new methods of micro and mass destruction to overcome his enemies.

Though currently presumed deceased because he'd been missing for some time, he turned up in Apex, and uses his deadly knowledge of creating toxic fumes to inflict mayhem on subjects that inhale them.

- **Tactical Ability: Nox Gas Trap**
- **Passive Ability: Nox Vision**
- **Ultimate Ability: Nox Gas Grenade**

GIBRALTAR

Makoa Gibraltar is known to most as the gentle giant, but also has a wild side that he can be known to unleash. As a shielded fortress, he helps get people out of dangerous situations. He learned and appreciates the value of helping others and has devoted his life to it.

Always a valuable asset to a team, Gibraltar shields his friends and allies from oncoming forces and incoming fire. As a rescuer by nature, he is happy to provide his services and will sacrifice himself for those that befriend him.

- **Tactical Ability: Dome of Protection**
- **Passive Ability: Gun Shield**
- **Ultimate Ability: Defensive Bombardment**

LIFELINE

Ajay Che is in it to win it, and she is never going to give up. As a combat medic, she is not your typical healer character. Ajay comes from a wealthy upbringing, but after learning that her family funded wars, she ran off to join a humanitarian cause and become committed to do some good in the world where help was needed.

She is sarcastic, fun, and callous and truly wants to make a difference in the world, even if things get bloody, though she is always up for healing her teammates in the push for victory.

- **Tactical Ability: D.O.C. Heal Drone**
- **Passive Ability: Combat Medic**
- **Ultimate Ability: Care Package**

MIRAGE – PURCHASE

A charismatic type that likes to stand out from the crowd, Mirage pushes limits and draws the attention of those around him. He's cocky and confident and does not mind causing a scene. As the youngest of four brothers, Elliott Witt stands out from those around him with more brains than brawn.

He works to outwit his opponents and charm anyone that comes into his path. He is smooth, debonair, and has many skills up his sleeve.

- **Tactical Ability: Psyche Out**
- **Passive Ability: Encore!**
- **Ultimate Ability: Vanishing Act**

OCTANE – PURCHASE

Everyone likes a good time and that's what Octavio Silva is made of – high-octane excitement. Always bored and set for life as the heir to a large pharmaceutical company, he entertained himself with adrenaline-rushing exploits that would defy death and give him the rush he was looking for.

After launching himself over a finish line using a grenade, he lost both his legs. That didn't stop him though. Ajay Che, the combat medic, fixed him up with new bionic legs to make him better, stronger, and faster.

- **Tactical Ability: Stim**
- **Passive Ability: Swift Mend**
- **Ultimate Ability: Launch Pad**

PATHFINDER

Pathfinder h-a-t-e-s losing, which is why he avoids it at all costs. MRVN is his real name and he was created for an unknown purpose by an unknown person, but he is not sure who or why. He has special scouting and surveying skills but doesn't know much else about himself.

Learning on the fly in his travels, he is drawn to people that give him hope and foster friendships. He is helpful and enthusiastic and ready to jump into the thick of a fight at a moment's notice.

- **Tactical Ability: Grappling Hook**
- **Passive Ability: Insider Knowledge**
- **Ultimate Ability: Zipline Gun**

WRAITH

After waking up in a mental facility with no memory of who she is or where she came from, Wraith has taken on a new purpose. A whirlwind fighter with many special powers, she is an interdimensional skirmisher that has inner voices that tell her what to do and how to do it.

With new powers constantly forming inside her, she continues to learn and become stronger. Wraith is a great ally as a teammate, but as an opponent she is not someone you want to cross.

- **Tactical Ability: Into the Void**
- **Passive Ability: Voices from the Void**
- **Ultimate Ability: Dimensional Rift**

You're free to choose any of the above characters when you play Apex Legends, though you will have to purchase the premium characters to use them. You can choose the same Legend or swap them every time you play the game.

PRACTICE MAKES PERFECT

It is most important that you practice often! This will help you develop new skills for your Legend, or learn how to do their finishing moves. Take the time to get comfortable with a certain character and you'll play at a higher level and have more success in your matches as a result.

One of the biggest tips we have when it comes to being successful in matches is to thoroughly learn and make use of your abilities whenever you can. Become familiar with them, learn when the best times to use them are, and practice until using their abilities become second nature.

Finally, be ready to exercise those abilities! If you wait too long your chance may never come and you may die without ever using them.

PATCH 1.1.1

Caustic and Gibraltar now have an additional passive called Fortified which reduces damage taken by 10 percent. We've also made some balance updates for Sniper Rifles, Havoc, Wingman, and Spitfire. Check out full patch notes by following @playapex on Twitter.

Ⓑ CLOSE

KINGS CANYON

GIBRALTAR
Use Dome of Protection to protect you and squad from your Mortar Strike in danger close situations.

BALANCING YOUR SQUAD

Balancing out your squad is a key to success. You cannot choose the classes that you are matched with when you're randomly playing against others online. However, there are times when you can invite your friends and they can choose classes that complement yours.

Among the best mixes of characters to put together is: Octane, Gibraltar, and Lifeline. Their skills play off of each other's, offering more vibrant gameplay. Octane will go in for the fight, while Lifeline tops off his health and Gibraltar helps protects him with his shields.

It is important that you consider the strengths and weaknesses of each player and then adjust the character each teammate uses accordingly.

Unfortunately, if your match is formed randomly through the server, you can't choose your teammates and will quickly realize if you have a good mix of characters or not. This is something to take note of when you go to play with your friends who can actually choose their characters before you join together to play as a team.

Characters can also be customized using many different skins and cosmetics that you can find or purchase in the game. These help you customize and individualize your characters much more than just choosing the specific character and class that you are playing with.

SKINS AND COSMETICS

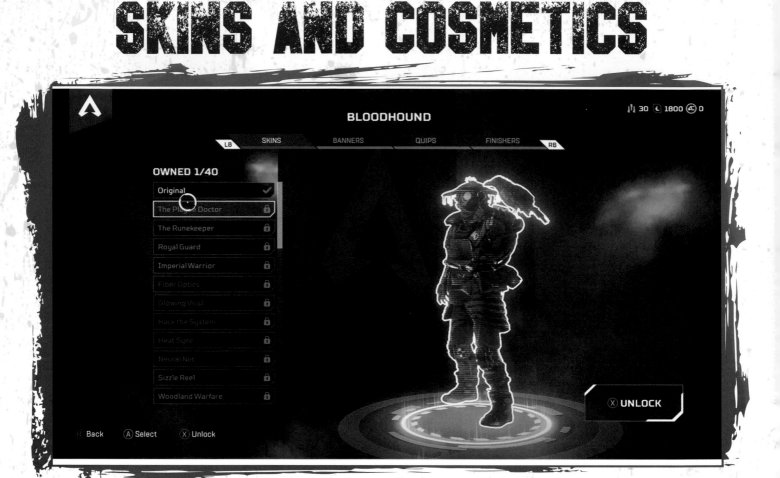

Having a good idea of what is available and knowing how to get skins and extras can help you customize your characters to the nines. Some skins and extras you can find in the game, others you might get from the Battle Pass, and still others you can just purchase on your own to customize your character with.

You can also craft custom skins using Crafting Metals right inside the game. If you're someone that loves customization and creating a highly specialized and extremely unique-looking character, then Apex Legends is definitely for you!

HOW TO GET SKINS

There are a few different ways you can get skins, and it partly depends on the character that you have.

The item shop should be your first stop for skins. You can choose from a bunch of different varieties, though not all the skins and customizations are available. Rare skins, or ones that have to be custom made, are not available in the shop. Apex Coins can be purchased to buy the items using your own real money through your account.

You can also earn items as a reward for playing the game or getting the Battle Pass. The game randomly hands out items to active players and those that are signed up and playing, or who are taking part in the Battle Pass, get their hands on the most exciting items.

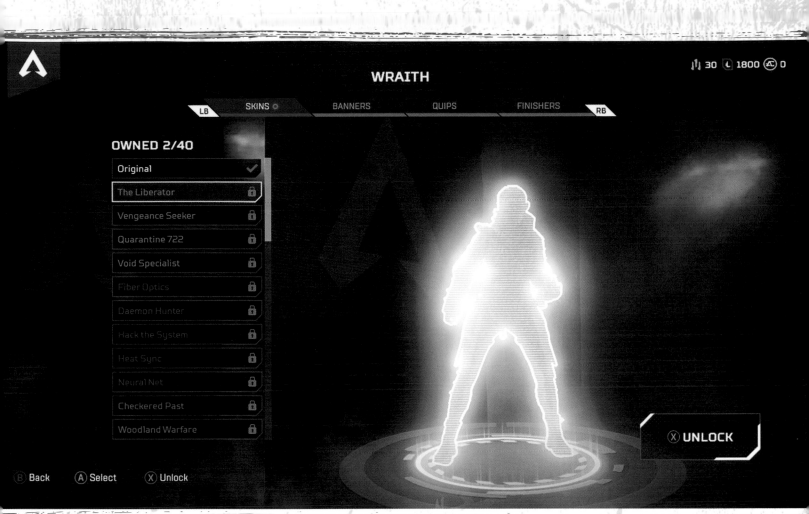

WRAITH

30   1800   0

LB   SKINS   BANNERS   QUIPS   FINISHERS   RB

OWNED 2/40

- Original ✓
- The Liberator 🔒
- Vengeance Seeker 🔒
- Quarantine 722 🔒
- Void Specialist 🔒
- Fiber Optics 🔒
- Daemon Hunter 🔒
- Hack the System 🔒
- Heat Sync 🔒
- Neural Net 🔒
- Checkered Past 🔒
- Woodland Warfare 🔒

(X) UNLOCK

(B) Back   (A) Select   (X) Unlock

Crafting Metals is another way you can get items. These are found in the Apex Packs, and it is random what comes inside Packs, but you can choose the rarity level that you want from the skin or item Pack.

LEGENDARY PACKS – 1,200 CRAFTING METALS

EPIC PACKS – 400 CRAFTING METALS

RARE PACKS – 60 CRAFTING METALS

COMMON PACKS – 30 CRAFTING METALS

SKINS LIST

There are numerous skins that you can purchase and find in the game. There are way too many to catalog here, so we provide you with an abridged collection of the awesome swag that is available. Remember, there are different levels for each skin and every player has a different skin for every level.

BLOODHOUND

LEGENDARY
- Royal Guard
- Imperial Warrior
- Plague Doctor
- Runekeeper

EPIC
- Heat Sync
- Fiber Optics
- Hack the System

GIBRALTAR

LEGENDARY
- Dark Side
- Ride or Die
- Millennium Tusk

EPIC
- Daemon Hunter
- Neural Net

LIFELINE

LEGENDARY
- London Calling
- Organized Anarchy
- Vital Signs

EPIC
- Blockchain Reaction
- Fiber Optics

RARE
- Revolutionary

OCTANE

LEGENDARY
- Gold Rush
- El Diablo
- Speed Demon
- Victory Lap

RARE
- Messenger

GIBRALTAR

🎖 30   ⏱ 1800   ⌾ 0

LB   **SKINS**   BANNERS   QUIPS   FINISHERS   RB

OWNED 1/40

- Original ✓
- Millennium Tusk 🔒
- Dark Side 🔒
- Ride or Die 🔒
- Bunker Buster 🔒
- Fiber Optics 🔒
- Daemon Hunter 🔒
- Hack the System 🔒
- Heat Sync 🔒
- Neural Net 🔒
- Molten Core 🔒
- Woodland Warfare 🔒

Ⓑ Back

Ⓧ UNLOCK

BANGALORE
LEGENDARY
- Apex Overdrive
- Officer Williams
- The Enforcer

EPIC
- Daemon Hunter
- Neural Net

CAUSTIC
LEGENDARY
- Blackheart
- Divine Right
- Sixth Sense
- Philosopher's Stone

EPIC
- Illegal Operation
- Heat Sync

MIRAGE
LEGENDARY
- Ghost Machine
- The Revenger
- The Prestige

EPIC
- Glowing Viral
- Fiber Optics

RARE
- Outlaw

PATHFINDER
LEGENDARY
- Angel City Pacer
- Model P
- Quicksilver
- The Aviator

EPIC
- Heat Sync
- User Friendly

WRAITH
LEGENDARY
- Quarantine 722
- The Liberator
- Void Specialist

EPIC
- Hack the System
- Fiber Optics

RARE
- Survivor

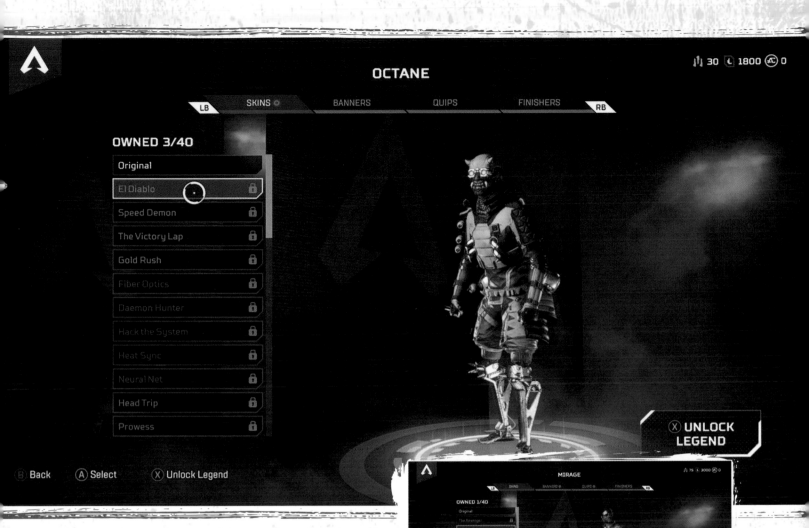

ALL THE BEST LOOT

There are many places to find loot in Apex. Loot is colored according to the level that it is graded as – white, blue, orange, and purple. Any areas of the map that have glowing blue on them is where loot is available and any gear that is lit up orange is the best loot available.

The best loot is not readily available when you first drop. This loot doesn't come out until the end of the match, which gives you something to look forward to if you can survive into the later stages of the match.

There is also the supply ship that provides a boatload of supplies. However, players should note that the ship is usually overrun by players in the beginning who are willing to fight to the death to get what they need off of the ship!

Get your hands on a **Kraber-1?**

That is one of the best weapons in the game thanks to its deadly damage output and accuracy. BUT, it takes forever to load, and good luck finding ammo for it because it is almost non-existent in the game! Use it wisely but sparingly.

Phoenix Packs are also in short supply, but highly sought after by many players. Tuck one in your inventory and hold onto it until you're down to a key moment in your match. Even if your team is losing big, it can turn the tables and might even help you win in the end.

Pinging items in your inventory is a great way to show your teammates which items you have a surplus of, and what you are low on, so you can redistribute key items amongst yourselves easily.

RARE HEIRLOOM ITEMS

There is literally a 1 in 500 chance of finding any of these items, so if you do, you're definitely going to want to pick it up and tuck it in your inventory.

There are rare banners, one-liners, and skins that can be found in the loot boxes that come in the Apex Pack. Items usually have a rarity "rating" attached to them and since these are heirloom items, they not only are rare, but they come with a backstory for the particular character that they drop for. They're bonus items that not everyone can get, so they're definitely a cool item to acquire and wield.

One of the best things about heirloom items is that it doesn't deduct from the space in your inventory, so it's almost like you're carrying nothing extra.

You cannot craft heirloom items, either, so don't try to overthink it. You just have to be one of the lucky few that get their hands on these items, and you'll either get one or you won't.

EA is reportedly preventing players from opening more than 500 Apex Packs if they do not get a heirloom set, so the more you grind, the more chances you'll have to find one.

Once you get an heirloom set, you won't get another until more of them are added to the game, since there are only so many that are released at any given moment.

There are many items throughout the game. Some that heal and help you, some that provide weapons of death and destruction, and some items even play off of each character's specific skillset, such as gasses for Caustic. These items have a huge impact on how you play Apex Legends and how far you get. The more you find, the better off you will be.

Taking the time to scour your surroundings while in a new area is ideal, but remember there are always enemies around you. Paying attention to who you come across and deciding whether to fight or flee is your first priority, items can wait until you have a moment of peace.

Making use of special items is not only important, but also exciting, as you never know what overall effect it is going to have. Whether it is a rare item, a cosmetic item, or an heirloom, finding new and exciting items and the almost infinite customization options is all part of the fun when you're playing this game.

Have you found any of those mythical items that can help make you a Legend?

WEAPONS

In any fighting game, you want to know as much as possible about the weapons available. Weapons in Apex are designed to provide a different feel and require different strategies and tactics to use most effectively.

Each weapon is geared towards a specific play style. This helps teach players new play styles and also helps them determine which weapons align best with the character they are currently using.

There are also hybrid weapons, which can be difficult to use for novices. The only way to get better at wielding hybrid weapons, or familiarizing yourself with any of the other items you find in the map, is by using Training Mode to test them out before heading into battle.

THE BEST GUNS IN APEX LEGENDS

There are so many guns, and so many variations of guns in this game that it takes time to find what really appeals to you. Here are our top rated and most beloved weapons of war in Apex Legends.

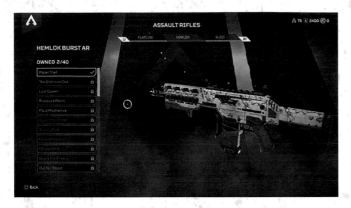

ASSAULT RIFLES

Rifles are found all around the map in nearly every match, because Apex is a battle game, after all. The first rifle that you will come across, the **R-301 Carbine,** is decent, but it is certainly not top of the line. It has a high accuracy rate, but doesn't do a lot of damage.

The next gun you will stumble upon is the **Hemlok Burst AR** which is easily able to fire three-round bursts designed to hit your opponent for more damage. There is a bit of kickback on this gun, but it isn't too bad. Many players prefer this weapon because of the burst feature.

A favorite for so many players is the **VK-47 Flatline** that is fully automatic, and provides stability and control while also having one of the best accuracy rates of all the assault rifles in the game. You can use it both close up, or at a fair distance away.

SNIPER RIFLES

There are four different sniper rifles you can get your hands on while playing the game. Of course, the top gun is the **Kraber .50-cal** for the awesome power and control. It is a Legendary weapon, holds only eight rounds, provides toggle and zoom, and can take down an enemy with just one shot.

The next sniper rifle is a semi-automatic **G7 Scout** which has some kickback and only holds six rounds, but still can get the job done. With good accuracy and quick firing power, it is a useful gun to have when you see another squad approaching from a distance.

The **Triple Threat** is at the same level as the G7, but it holds only five rounds. You can choose which you like the best from these two by giving them both a try.

PISTOLS

Having a handgun is not a bad thing when it comes to close-range encounters. Among the most powerful of these is the **Mozambique shotgun-pistol**. It is quite powerful, and dangerous. With a bodyshot damage of 45 and a headshot damage of 66, you can truly take someone down hard and fast in close quarters.

The next on the list and a player favorite, is the **Wingman,** a classic revolver that packs a lot of punch. It holds six rounds and can knock nearby enemies down easily, efficiently, and quickly. You can also reload and fire in one swift move.

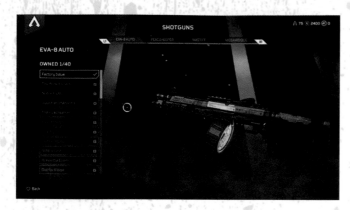

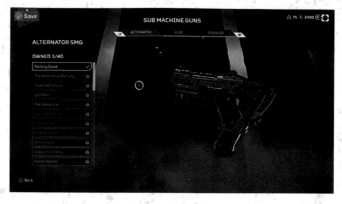

SHOTGUNS

Everyone loves a little shotgun action in their battle game, and Apex Legends embraces these powerful short-range weapons. **The Mastiff Legendary Shotgun** is among the most sought-after guns despite having the kickback of a mule because of its accurate, devastating blow. You can blast your opponents out of the way with literally one click. They are hard to come by, but if you find one, hang on tight because it will come in handy on your way to victory.

Further down the list but then also easier to find, is the semi-automatic **EVA-8 Auto**—a shotgun that can quickly fire but maintains solid stability. It is less powerful than the Mastiff, but easy to use and can help you get out of a jam without having to fumble with a trigger.

SMGS

Similar to a pistol with a similar fire pattern, the **Alternator SMG** fires more slowly than other SMG options but offers impressive aim for players that treasure accuracy. If you pick up the R-99, you will notice that it doesn't fire as straight at the Alternator.

If you want to do the most damage in the shortest period of time, the Prowler is the SMG for you. You can rapidly burst five rounds out of the **Prowler Burst PDW.** Do a lot of damage and have the best aim when using this futuristic action gun.

LMGS

There are only two of these guns out there, so keep on the lookout for these bad boys.

A highly sought after weapon, the **M600 Spitfire** is fully automatic and has the highest accuracy with a decent amount of damage. It reloads fast and brings a lot of gun to the fight when you are either trying to dominate or escape a confrontation.

The other LMG on the list is the **Devotion.** This gun requires a bit more aim and steadiness to be effective. It is fully-automatic and uses energy ammo. Its fire rate will increase over time with use. The shot pattern can drift when firing it, so it is not the most stable gun, but with some practice, you will find that you can deal some pretty nasty damage with this baby.

WEAPON CHART AND DAMAGE DEALT

Players can never have enough knowledge about the weapons available to them and their enemies on the field of play, so here's more data on each of the weapons found in Apex Legends. You might be surprised to learn that some guns are much more powerful than others even though they look similar.

**Tip – When you find any of the guns listed below, they will come without any attachments. If you find any attachments, you can easily add them.

If the guns are glowing gold, this does not mean that they are Legendary. This actually means that they are a rare spawn. These spawns already have the top tier attachments on the gun for you to use!

There are currently only two Legendary weapons in the whole game, the **Kraber .50 Cal Sniper** and the **Mastiff Shotgun.**

PISTOLS

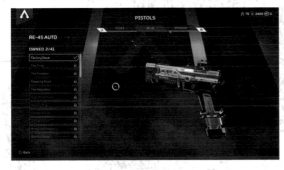

RE-45 AUTO

SPECS
- Fast Shooting
- You Control Recoil
- Light Rounds
- Holds 15 Rounds
- Fully Automatic

SLOTS
- Barrel Attachment
- Optic Attachment
- Mag Attachment

DAMAGE
- Bodyshot: 11 damage, 132 DPS
- Headshot: 16 damage, 192 DPS

P2020

SPECS
- Standard pistol
- Light Rounds
- Holds 10 Rounds
- Semi Automatic

SLOTS
- Optic Attachment
- Mag Attachment

DAMAGE
- Bodyshot: 12 damage, 84 DPS
- Headshot: 18 damage, 126 DPS

WINGMAN

SPECS
- Standard Desert Eagle Pistol
- Great Aim
- Heavy Rounds
- Holds 4 Rounds
- High Power Revolver

SLOTS
- Optic Attachment
- Mag Attachment
- Hop Up Attachment

DAMAGE
- Bodyshot: 45 damage, 135 DPS
- Headshot: 90 damage, 270 DPS

SHOTGUNS

EVA-8 AUTO

SPECS
- Fast Shooting
- Shotgun Shells
- Holds 8 Rounds
- Repeated Firing Power
- Fully Automatic

SLOTS
- Optic Attachment
- Mag Attachment

DAMAGE

The damage depends on where on the body and how many are landed there of the target. Each land deals 7-damage on the body and 10-damage to the head area. There are 9 pellets per round, per shot.

- Bodyshot: 63 damage, 126 DPS
- Headshot: 90 damage, 180 DPS

MASTIFF SHOTGUN

SPECS
- Fires in a Horizontal Line
- Can't Be Reloaded
- Legendary
- Semi Automatic

DAMAGE

The damage depends on where on the body and how many are landed there of the target. Each land deals 18-damage on the body and 36-damage to the head area. There are 8 pellets per round, per shot.

- Bodyshot: 144 damage, 144 DPS
- Headshot: 288 damage, 288 DPS

MOZAMBIQUE SHOTGUN

SPECS
- Pistol and a Shotgun
- Shotgun Shells
- Holds 3 Rounds
- Triple Barrel Shotgun Pistol

SLOTS
- Optic Attachment
- Mag Attachment

DAMAGE
- Bodyshot: 45 damage, 135 DPS
- Headshot: 66 damage, 198 DPS

PEACEKEEPER

SPECS
- Standard Shotgun
- Shotgun Shells
- Holds 6 Rounds
- Lever Action Shotgun

SLOTS
- Optic Attachment
- Mag Attachment
- Hop Up Attachment

DAMAGE

The damage depends on where on the body and how many shots actually strike the target. Each strike deals 10-damage on the body and 15-damage to the head area. There are 11 pellets per round, per shot.

- Bodyshot: 110 damage, 110 DPS
- Headshot: 165 damage, 165 DPS

SMGS

ALTERNATOR SMG

SPECS
- Slow Firing
- Looks Like a Pistol
- Light Ammo
- Holds 16 Rounds
- Twin Barrel, Full Auto

SLOTS
- Barrel Attachment
- Optic Attachment
- Mag Attachment
- Stock Attachment

DAMAGE
- Bodyshot: 13 damage, 139 DPS
- Headshot: 19 damage, 203 DPS

PROWLER BURST PDW

SPECS
- Like a P-90
- Fires 5-Round Bursts
- Heavy Rounds
- Holds 20 Rounds
- Gives 4 Shots Total
- 5-Round Burst

SLOTS
- Optic Attachment
- Mag Attachment
- Stock Attachment
- Hop Up Attachment

DAMAGE
- Bodyshot: 14 damage or 70 if you get all shots, 186 DPS
- Headshot: 21 damage or 105 if you get all shots, 279 DPS

R-99

SPECS
- Standard SMG
- Quickly Fires
- Low Damage Per Bullet
- Light Rounds
- Holds 18 Rounds
- Rapid Fire Automatic

SLOTS
- Barrel Attachment
- Optic Attachment
- Mag Attachment
- Stock Attachment

DAMAGE
- Bodyshot: 12 damage, 216 DPS
- Headshot: 18 damage, 324 DPS

ASSAULT RIFLES

HAVOC RIFLE

SPECS
- Similar to the Devotion
- Charge Beam Alt-Fire Mode
- Energy Ammo
- Fully Automatic, Charged

SLOTS
- Optic Attachment
- Stock Attachment
- Hop Up Attachment

DAMAGE
- Bodyshot: 18 damage
- Headshot: 36 damage

HEMLOK BURST AR

SPECS
- Burst Rifle
- Looks Like a Pistol
- Heavy Rounds
- Holds 18 Rounds
- Shoots 3 Rounds Per Shot
- Burst Assault Rifle

SLOTS
- Barrel Attachment
- Optic Attachment
- Mag Attachment
- Stock Attachment

DAMAGE
- Bodyshot: 18 damage or 54 if the full burst hits, 144 DPS
- Headshot: 24 damage or 72 if the full burst hits, 288 DPS

R-301 CARBINE

SPECS
- Mix of an Assault Rifle and SMG
- Accurate with Lower Damage
- High Accuracy
- Light Ammo
- Holds 18 Rounds
- Full Auto

SLOTS
- Barrel Attachment
- Optic Attachment
- Mag Attachment
- Stock Attachment

DAMAGE
- Bodyshot: 14 damage, 186 DPS
- Headshot: 28 damage, 336 DPS

VK-47 FLATLINE

SPECS
- Standard Assault Rifle
- Strong Damage
- Heavy Rounds
- Holds 20 Rounds
- Full Auto

SLOTS
- Optic Attachment
- Mag Attachment
- Stock Attachment

DAMAGE
- Bodyshot: 16 damage, 160 DPS
- Headshot: 32 damage, 320 DPS
- Bodyshot: 110 damage, 110 DPS
- Headshot: 165 damage, 165 DPS

LMGS

DEVOTION

SPECS
- Speeds Up the Longer You Hold the Trigger
- Energy Ammo
- Full Auto

SLOTS
- Barrel Attachment
- Optic Attachment
- Stock Attachment
- Hop Up Attachment

DAMAGE
- Bodyshot: 17 damage, 255 DPS
- Headshot: 34 damage, 510 DPS

M600 SPITFIRE

SPECS
- Accurate
- Reasonable Fire Rate, Solid Damage
- Heavy Rounds
- Holds 35 Rounds
- Quick Reload Time
- Full Auto

SLOTS
- Barrel Attachment
- Optic Attachment
- Mag Attachment
- Stock Attachment

DAMAGE
- Bodyshot: 18 damage
- Headshot: 36 damage

SNIPER RIFLES

G7 SCOUT

SPECS
- Quick Firing
- Versatile Sniper
- Mid to Long Range Shooting
- Light Rounds
- Holds 10 Rounds
- Semi Auto

SLOTS
- Barrel Attachment
- Optic Attachment
- Mag Attachment
- Stock Attachment

DAMAGE
- Bodyshot: 30 damage, 120 DPS
- Headshot: 60 damage, 250 DPS

KRABER .50-CAL SNIPER

SPECS
- Legendary
- 1 Hit Kill
- Holds 8 Rounds
- 4 Per Magazine, 2 Magazines Per Gun

- Bolt Action Sniper Rifle
- 6x – 10x Variable
- Cannot Be Reloaded

DAMAGE
- Bodyshot: 125 damage, 125 DPS
- Headshot: 250 damage, 250 DPS

LONGBOW DMR

SPECS
- Standard Sniper Rifle
- Holds 5 Rounds
- Semi Auto

SLOTS
- Barrel Attachment
- Optic Attachment
- Mag Attachment
- Stock Attachment
- Hop Up Attachment

DAMAGE
- Bodyshot: 55 damage, 55 DPS
- Headshot: 110 damage, 110 DPS

TRIPLE TAKE

SPECS
- Fires One Round, Three Projectiles
- Energy Ammo
- Holds 5 Rounds
- Triple Barrel Sniper Rifle
- Upgrade with Precision Choke

SLOTS
- Optic Attachment
- Stock Attachment
- Hop Up Attachment

DAMAGE
- Bodyshot: 69 damage, 69 DPS
- Headshot: 138 damage, 138 DPS

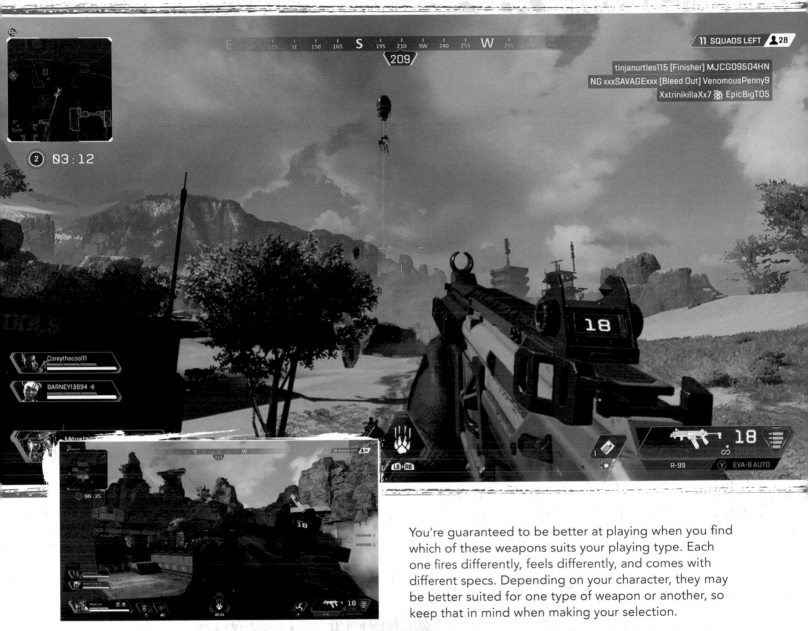

You're guaranteed to be better at playing when you find which of these weapons suits your playing type. Each one fires differently, feels differently, and comes with different specs. Depending on your character, they may be better suited for one type of weapon or another, so keep that in mind when making your selection.

The best way to find the perfect weapon for you and your play style is to test out each option in Practice Mode. Try them out and decide what you like the best before pushing the limits in matches. Practice Mode is where you can see exactly what is available, how it looks, and become familiar with how to use it.

ARMOR

The armor that you choose to wear makes a huge difference on how difficult you are to kill, so always be on the lookout for the best pieces, upgrade whenever possible, and you'll find it much easier to stay alive through intense combat.

There are many different types of armor that you can find sprinkled throughout the map to help you stay alive longer. Just like guns, armor pieces have different rarities and power levels, making some pieces far more useful than others in certain situations.

The rarity and quality of the items are color coded, so this can make things easier when trying to find the best gear and armor to use.

WHITE – COMMON
BLUE – RARE
PURPLE – EPIC
GOLD – LEGENDARY

Since these items spawn at different locations all the time, there is really no way to recommend where to go or when to go there to find them. You just have to hope you stumble across something that you're able to use.

LEGENDARY GEAR IN APEX LEGENDS

The quality jump between Epic and Legendary is different from the jump in the other quality items. Both Epic and Legendary items boast the same stat values, but Legendary items offer something extra for the user to enjoy.

All Legendary items are considered to be Level 4 items.

BODY SHIELD
- +100 Shield Protection
- Fully Recharges After Executing Enemy

HELMET
- 25% Damage Reduction
- Increases Charge Speed of Both Tactical and Ultimate Abilities

KNOCKDOWN SHIELD
- 750 Health Knockdown Shield
- Self-Revives Once if Knocked

BACKPACK
- Adds 6 Inventory Slots
- Healing Items Only Take Half the Time to Consume and Work

BODY SHIELDS

These are what is going to protect you when the time comes to block enemy attacks. If you have a shield on, they have to fight their way through that before they can deal any damage to your actual character, which buys you more time.

The quality of the shield will be shown in the smaller bars above your health bar. The more shield bars you have, the better protection your shield provides.

LEVEL 1 – COMMON
+50 Shield Protection

LEVEL 2 – RARE
+75 Shield Protection

LEVEL 3 – EPIC
+100 Shield Protection

LEVEL 4 – LEGENDARY
+100 Shield Protection
Fully Recharges Shields Upon Executing Enemy

HELMETS

This is a type of armor that you can equip your character with while playing in the game, though they work a bit differently than what you might expect. Instead of providing you with extra health, they allow you to absorb less damage when you're hit with a headshot, making it more difficult for precise enemies to beat you.

There's a catch though, because the reductions in the amount of damage dealt by a headshot is only taken from the bonus headshot and not the total damage from the headshot.

For example:

If you have made a headshot from a Wingman, it would give 45 body shot damage and then another 45 head damage that is acting as a bonus shot. This means you get a total of 90 damage dealt.

However, if someone with a white helmet is hit, you'd think you dealt 77 damage to the person when they use the helmet, when in fact, you actually do 81. In short, helmets offer a bit of protection, but not as much as you might expect after looking at damage reduction stats.

LEVEL 1 – COMMON
10% Damage Reduction

LEVEL 2 – RARE
20% Damage Reduction

LEVEL 3 – EPIC
25% Damage Reduction

LEVEL 4 – LEGENDARY
25% Damage Reduction
Increases Charge Speed of Tactical and Ultimate Abilities

KNOCKDOWN SHIELDS

These were originally introduced because of Apex Legend's focus on squads and teamwork. After being killed by an enemy you simply get knocked down and there is an opportunity for your teammates to revive you. A knockdown shield can help you at this time.

If you're knocked, you can crawl around on the ground, open and close doors, and even communicate with your team members, but you cannot take part in battles with them until you're restored.

If you have a knockdown shield equipped, you're able to activate it by holding your right mouse clicker down. This opens up a curved shield that protects you from oncoming bullets. The number of hit points that you have is shown on the screen.

This is only going to protect from outside fire. If an enemy notices that you're down, they can come over and perform their execution move on you to eliminate you entirely from the game. As such, you want to stay as far away from them as possible if you have been knocked and hide until you're able to be revived back into the game.

LEVEL 1 – COMMON
100 Health Shield

LEVEL 2 – RARE
250 Health Shield

LEVEL 3 – EPIC
750 Health Shield

LEVEL 4 – LEGENDARY
750 Health Shield
Self-Revive Once Knocked

***YOUR SHIELDS WILL RECHARGE IF YOU HIDE AND LET THEM! THEY WILL BOOST BACK UP!

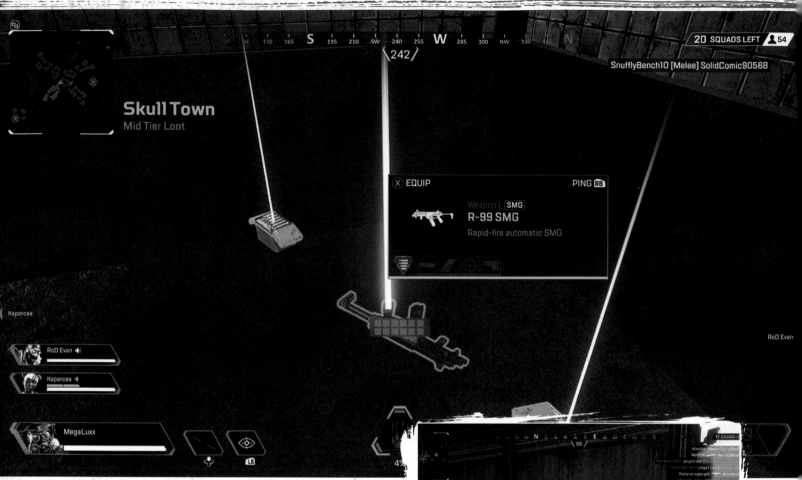

Skull Town
Mid Tier Loot

X EQUIP   PING RB

Weapon | SMG
R-99 SMG
Rapid-fire automatic SMG.

20 SQUADS LEFT   54
SnufflyBench10 [Melee] SolidComic90568

Kapercea

RoD Evan

Kapercea

MegaLuxx

BACKPACKS

Backpacks are one of the most useful pieces of gear/armor you can get in the game. You will want to try to find one as soon as you land, because the sooner you get one, the more use you can extract from it during gameplay.

You're able to unlock more inventory slots when you find one and equip it. This helps when you come across stuff that you want to keep with you, but perhaps currently do not have enough space and need to choose what to keep and what to get rid of.

Also, a warning: If you drop a backpack full of stuff during the game, all of the items inside will fall to the ground, making them available for anyone nearby to grab. Hold onto your backpack!

LEVEL 1 – COMMON
+2 Inventory Slots

LEVEL 2 – RARE
+4 Inventory Slots

LEVEL 3 – EPIC
+6 Inventory Slots

LEVEL 4 – LEGENDARY
+6 Inventory Slots
Healing Items Take Only Half Time to Consume and Work

If you're not wearing any armor, put on whatever you find first. Any armor is better than nothing, and each additional piece will make you more effective out on the battlefield.

Many of the armor items are easier to find than weapons, so grab and use them whenever you can. If you already have an item always ping your teammates, as maybe they can use it.

Wearing good armor is a key to survival in Apex, so be on the lookout for upgrades wherever and whenever possible.

USEFUL GEAR AND EXTRAS

There's a ton of gear and other stuff to find in Apex Legends. When you're playing, you generally want to grab items whenever you can. The ability to identify the object and know how it works is critical to help you make the best use of whatever you come across.

Healing items should be familiar for fans of this type of game. The shield system does change because you cannot use a shield charger without having one of the armor types listed above. This system allows you to continuously recharge your shield using the extra attachments and batteries you find.

You can also get the Ultimate Ability, which is a departure from other games, because you generally cannot pick up abilities as if they are gear or extras.

Read on to learn more about all of them and find out what you have and what you need to make it to the end of the game and come out a Legend!

HEALING ITEMS

Healing items provide many benefits. Not only can you hide and heal, but you can also "equip" them and heal more slowly over time while you move strategically. You can also use them on team members. There are many ways to use healing items but one thing is for certain, don't ever pass them by when you see them!

SYRINGE
- +25 Health
- 5 Second Use Time
- Basic Bandage

MED KIT
- +100 Health
- 8 Second Use Time
- Standard Big Heal

PHOENIX KIT
- +100 Health
- +100 Shields
- 10 Second Use Time
- Fully Restores Both Your Health and Shields
- Epic Rarity

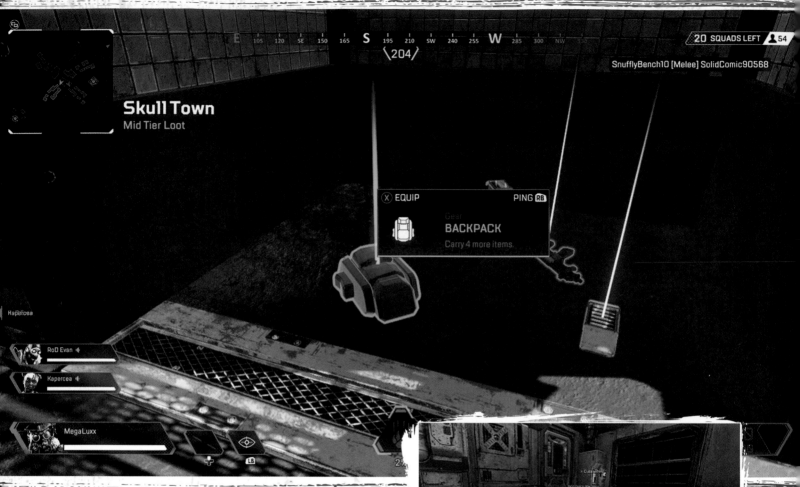

SHIELD ADDITIONS

You can find additions throughout the game map. A lot of these additions can help not only with your health, but also with your shield. If you have armor that provides a protective layer, then these additions are extra valuable. Keep them charged up, stay on the offensive, and maximize your protection when you find any of these extras.

SHIELD CELL

- +25 Shields
- 3 Second Use Time
- Lowest Tier Shield Charge

SHIELD BATTERY

- +100 Shields
- 5 Second Use Time
- Big Shield Recharge
- Doesn't Matter Shield Capacity

ULTIMATE ACCELERANT

- +20% Ultimate Energy
- 7 Second Use Time
- Boosts Energy to Use it Quicker
- Use Immediately

WEAPON ATTACHMENTS AND EXTRAS

There are also attachments and extras that you can place on your weapons. These can boost the damage that is dealt by the weapons, while also making the weapons usable for longer periods of time. Some will even make your aim better and your shot sharper.

When you find the attachments, which will be laying around everywhere, like the other drops in the game, you can hover over them to see if they can be fitted to your particular weapon. If they can, you can click on them and they will add to the weapon or replace any others that might not be as good.

All of the attachments have different types of benefits that come with them. Depending on the gun and attachment that you have, you can find that you're grabbing the right addition to add to your gun. Some of the attachments can only be found in specific colors, like gold, so this is something to keep in mind. They'll be less likely to find.

Learn more about these attachments, so when you come across them, you will see just how much good they can do for you.

HOP UP ATTACHMENTS

Hop Ups can only be fitted on a handful of guns, so it is important that you have the right weapon for this attachment. They come with excellent benefits and are a must-have accessory for anyone who wants to add a bit more punch to their weapon. They are only available in purple and gold colors, so this means they provide a lot of benefit but are also harder to find.

PRECISION CHOKE
Use this on the: Peacekeeper, Triple Take
Ability: Holds ADS for a tighter spread over time

SELECTFIRE RECEIVER
Use this on the: Prowler, Havoc
Ability: Enables full-auto firing mode

SKULLPIERCER RIFLING
Use this on the: Longbow – Wingman
Ability: Increases headshot damage

TURBOCHARGER
Use this on the: Devotion, Havoc
Ability: Reduces or removes spin up time

BARREL ATTACHMENTS

Used to reduce the recoil on the weapons that you have, they are most helpful for fast-firing, higher recoil guns that require more precision.

BARREL STABILIZER

- LMGs, RE 45, G7 Scout, Longbow, Alternator, R-99, Hemlok, R-301 Carbine

- White, Blue, Purple, Gold

- Reduces Recoil

- Gold – Reduces Weapon Flash

OPTIC ATTACHMENTS

If you want a longer range of sight for your weapon, especially on those sniper weapons, then optic attachments are just what you need. They come in different types with various attributes such as extra zoom or low-lighting.

One unique thing about these scopes is that if you get one in gold, you can actually have the enemies highlighted using the Threat Highlighting feature that comes on them. They are lit up in red and you can see them clearly in the distance.

1X HALO

- All Weapons
- White
- Close Ranged Sight

1X DIGITAL THREAT

- Shotguns, SMGs, Pistols
- Gold
- Close Ranged Sight with Threat Detection

1-2X VARIABLE HALO

- All Weapons
- Blue
- Close Ranged Variable Sight

1X HCOG CLASSIC

- All Weapons
- White
- Close Ranged Sight

1X HCOG BRUISER
- All Weapons
- Blue
- Close Ranged Sight

1X HCOG RANGER
- Snipers, SMGs, LMGs, ARs
- Purple
- Mid-Ranged Sight

2-4X VARIABLE AOG
- Snipers, SMGs, LMGs, ARs
- Purple
- Mid-Ranged Variable Sight

6X SNIPER
- Snipers
- Blue
- Long Ranged Sight

4-8X VARIABLE SNIPER
- Snipers
- Purple
- Long Ranged Variable Sight

4-10X DIGITAL SNIPER THREAT
- Snipers
- Gold
- Long Ranged Variable Sight with Threat Detection

MAG ATTACHMENTS

The main benefit of having these attachments is to increase the magazine size of your gun. This will help you get more shots in and not have to worry about switching weapons or finding time to reload. Some of these offer a bit more than size though, they can also deliver faster firing rates or reload times!

EXTENDED LIGHT MAG
- All Light Weapons
- White, Blue, Purple, Gold
- Increases Ammo Capacity
- Blue, Purple, Gold: Reduces Reload Time

EXTENDED HEAVY MAG
- All Heavy Weapons
- White, Blue, Purple, Gold
- Increases Ammo Capacity
- Blue, Purple, Gold: Reduces Reload Time

SHOTGUN BOLT
- Shotguns
- White, Blue, Purple, Gold
- Increases Fire Rate

STOCK ATTACHMENTS

Reduce the draw time of your weapon when you use the stock attachments that can slip right on. It can also reduce the amount of aim drift that you have, which happens more often than not when aiming down sights. Improve your accuracy with an attachment that helps your aim.

STANDARD STOCK

- LMGs, SMGs, ARs
- White, Blue, Purple, Gold
- Decreases the Draw Time
- Reduces Aim Drift

SNIPER STOCK

- Snipers
- White, Blue, Purple, Gold
- Decreases Draw Time
- Reduces Aim Drift

THE GOLD BARREL STABILIZER

While this is not really a piece of armor, it is still an add-on for armor that can be found hidden somewhere on the map. This stabilizer reduces the flash that your weapon makes while also blunting the amount of damage reduction that you absorb when your weapon recoils.

With so many attachments and extras to make use of to enhance your combat and defensive abilities in battle, there's literally something for everyone in Apex Legends. Just make sure you're getting the most out of your attachments and weapons by learning what they do. It is also critical to understand how they may work in concert with one another to ensure that you are getting the maximum performance out of them in giving yourself an edge over your enemies.

OFFENSIVE TACTICS

Tactics: (Urban Dictionary) tac·tic /ˈtaktik/ noun
To overcome a sticky situation using unorthodox and
sometimes extreme techniques. -Josh, November 12, 2003

There is no way around it: everyone that plays video games, from the Noobs to the Pros use tactics. Even if you aren't aware of it, it's happening. Offensive or defensive, from your choice of character to the location you choose to land, even what you pick up and add to your backpack will all factor into your offensive or defensive strength! This section will break down tactics into the two most basic categories: Offensive and Defensive. We will do the hard stuff for you – all you need to do is decide whether you want to be an aggressive, in-your-face player like Bloodhound, or an upbeat medic that loves to give you defensive "Birthday Presents" like Lifeline, and by the end of this chapter you'll be ready to start your journey to become a Champion of the Arena.

OFFENSIVE: LET'S GET AGGRESSIVE. THE TOP OFFENSIVE CHARACTERS.

Your first step in conquering the arena is helping create a balanced team by picking a player that will amplify any missing elements. For example, Lifeline, Wraith, and Bangalore would be a well-balanced group; you have your aggressiveness in Bangalore, the defensive capacities of Lifeline, and the unique nature of Wraith that can flip from offensive to defensive. Focusing on the offense right now, you should consider choosing any of the following characters:

THE ORIGINALS

- **BANGALORE** (Professional Soldier)
  "Come get some."

- **BLOODHOUND** (Technological Tracker)
  "Honor the Allfather."

- **WRAITH** (Interdimensional Skirmisher)
  "Try not to blink."

THE UNLOCKABLE:

- **MIRAGE** (Holographic Trickster)
  "You got Bamboozled."

- **THE NEW KID** – First additional character added for the season pass

- **OCTANE** (High Speed Daredevil)
  "I do this for the rush."

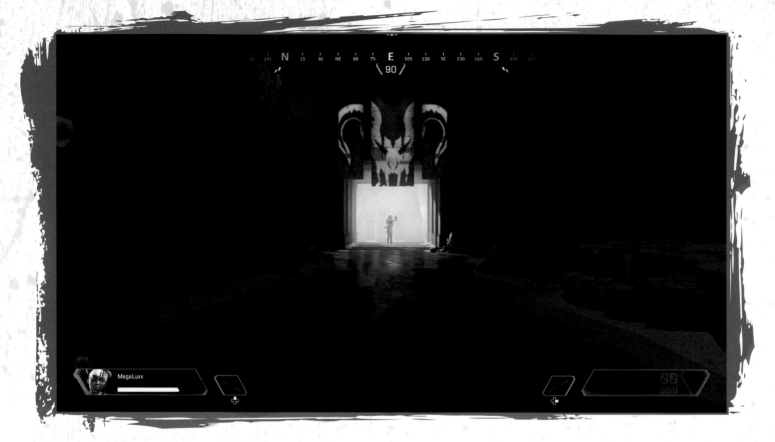

Mirage and Wraith are very interesting characters as they ride the line between offensive and defensive. Depending on how you play with them (we will touch on this further into tactics) they can act as the wildcard of the team, filling in offensive or defensive holes as you need to. Keep in mind; any of these characters can be used as offensive or defensive. This is just to help sort those that are more aggressive from the group.

BREAKING IT DOWN
BANGALORE

Bangalore has some very useful special abilities that allow her to claim a place in the offensive character roster. Her passive ability is called Double Time. This allows her to move faster while taking fire during a sprint for a short time. In offensive strategy this can help you position Bangalore closer to the enemy for an aggressive attack during a firefight, or to draw fire from offensively weaker players / characters.

Her Tactical ability is Smoke Launcher. This ability fires a high velocity smoke canister that explodes into a smoke wall on impact. Perfect for confusing opponents, this smoke wall can allow you to either rush the opposition or reposition for a sneak attack. If used in combination with Wraith's portals, this is a very effective offensive tactic for positioning, and can help in situations where another team (or teams) is/are trying to third party you.

Finally, Bangalore's ultimate ability, Rolling Thunder. This ultimate calls in an artillery strike that slowly creeps across the landscape, blowing up everything in its path. Be sure to get out of its way! It isn't picky about who it takes out. Rolling Thunder is an extremely valuable gift in an offensively charged match as it can affect multiple teams. This is especially useful near the end of the game, when multiple parties are battling in a small, contained area.

BLOODHOUND

Bloodhound is an extremely dangerous offensive player. Because of his ability to outline enemies and see their footsteps to determine location, a good Bloodhound can use his tools to locate and hunt mercilessly. He offers an excellent advantage in staying two steps ahead of your enemies.

Bloodhound's passive ability is Tracker. Foes leave clues all over the place, and Bloodhound is the man to find them. This offers a great offensive advantage by giving you the ability to see the direction your opponents went and to scan terrain to find optimal ambush sites.

The tactical ability belonging to Bloodhound is Eye of the Allfather. This briefly reveals enemies, traps, and clues through all structures in front of you. While this is optimal for defense, it is also quite handy for offense in that it can help you plot the safest course to your enemy to launch an attack, while helping you keep your team safe at the same time.

Finally, his ultimate ability, Beast of the Hunt, turns Bloodhound into a lethal predator. With enhanced senses that allow you to see cold tracks and the ability to move faster he turns into something no enemy team will want to mess with. He is able to stalk his prey after they leave your direct vicinity.

BurlyBasil78981

OCTANE

The newest character added to the Apex Legends roster, Octane is a self-proclaimed high speed daredevil. A virtual loose cannon, Octane is not above hurting himself to get the kills, which makes him an impressive offensive player. Octane is a rogue. If you prefer to play offensively in a more solo capacity, he has the speed, dexterity, and cunning to take out full squads single-handedly.

The hands down fastest and most agile of the characters at the time of writing, Octane is incredibly valuable in an aggressive and offensive campaign. He is always down for a challenge and ready to stir up a fight. Octane's passive ability is very handy in an offensive campaign. Swift Mend restores his health over time while he isn't taking damage. This can allow him to pop in and out, knocking off a few challengers and then speeding off to heal.

His tactical ability is Stim. Octane gleefully stabs himself with the stim, granting 30% more speed for 6 seconds. Like any other green, glowing, nuclear type of ooze you may put into your body, this stim has a negative effect and causes Octane's health to wane. This ability also reduces the effects of anything that would normally slow down a character.

Finally, Octane's ultimate ability, The Launch Pad. Imagine a much more dangerous, and high intensity trampoline, Octane style. This pad will catapult users through the air, which in an offensive setting, can land your entire team in the middle of unsuspecting wannabe champions, trying to get their loot on.

When you are heading into a firefight, and seeking out danger, these perks can prove invaluable, making Octane, if used correctly, a one man wrecking machine.

Something to keep in mind no matter who you choose as your player – in an offensive situation, be sure to knock all players on a team before you attempt to kill them. Killing someone that is already knocked is a dangerous ploy as it makes you a target for their healthy teammates. Also, once a team is knocked they instantly die.

THE MAP. YOUR DROP SPOT.

After you choose your character, the next thing your team will do is pick the drop spot. Even if you aren't the jumpmaster, this section can help you maximize the map, and location points that are vital for offensive play.

JUMPMASTER

As an offensive jumpmaster, your job is deciding where to enter the battle. You want to land in the most prime loot areas. Some of these locations are found on the map, highlighted by a blue circle (high tier loot area). Certain locations are almost always guaranteed to offer you tons of great, high tier loot (hot zones), for example: The Drop Ship, Skulltown, Slum Lakes, the Bunker, Relay, Artillery, Hydrodam, and the Air Base.

Here's how to hit these locations and maneuver yourself into great offensive positioning.

THE DROP SHIP

There will always be loot located on the front and tail of the ship, as well as the inside. Your best bet when jumping here is to hit the nose or tail, grabbing everything you can. Even if you don't think you need it, this will prevent other teams (and there will be other teams) from getting it. Work your way in from there, but be on guard. This is a very hot drop area. The Drop Ship glides along until reaching a certain location, and then parks. If you are the last team standing on board, this is great offensive positioning, allowing you to come off the ship locked and loaded and ready to mow down unfortunate teams.

SKULLTOWN

A ton of buildings and rooftops dominate Skulltown. It's best to land on the edge of this X shaped landmark, and work your way to the center, or from one end to the other. Another great plan would be landing directly on one of the rooftops, and jump from one roof to another as there is abundant loot on these roofs.

SLUM LAKES

Slum Lakes has the offensive benefit of a preplaced zipline that can take you from one end of the town to the other in a manner of moments. It's a straight-forward town; lots of little buildings and not much rooftop action, although you can be rewarded by following zip lines into the trees filling the swampy areas. Very close to the edge of the map, Slum Lake offers the benefit of knowing there will be very few if any enemies behind you. The way the buildings are laid out makes it easy to go from one door to another and offers plenty of ambush spots. If setting up an ambush isn't your offensive style, the zipline is a very fun and unexpected way to "drop in" on other players, since you are able to jump off any time you want.

THE BUNKER

With only two entrances and two exits, this narrow hallway full of adjacent rooms demands your offensive game be on point. This location is pretty self-explanatory. Work your way from one end to the other, looting as you go and decimating enemies along the way. You can either flush prey into the building and trap them there, or chase them out, trap them inside or wait for them at the exit, Depending on the characters you have chosen, you will approach this differently, but will be able to tackle this offensively no matter which way you choose to play it.

ARTILLERY

This base connects to other parts of the map with a tunnel. At the very top of the map, there is no way for you to be surrounded if you land here. It has two very tall buildings in the back that can be looted from bottom up, and if you are standing on top you can see the entire area, making it a valuable location to spot enemies and, using the ping system, take them out. A good offensive strategy in landing here would be to hit the two long buildings on the ground in front, move forward to the containers, go left or right to those buildings, then proceed to the two all the way at the back, looting from bottom to top as mentioned before. Once at the top, survey the area, and if you aren't in the circle, you can use the tunnel to shift to another location.

RELAY

Located in the top right corner of the map, Relay also keeps enemies off your back. With a series of zip lines running throughout the area, Relay is easy to get around, and offers many surprise drop points to gain the advantage on other teams. There is no other town on the map that offers such an elaborate series of zip lines.

HYDRODAM

Hydrodam takes up a wide footprint on the map, and gives you a lot of aerial views to plot the demise of challengers. It is easy to access 3 or 4 other locations after you loot here. After you jump down, loot the bunker. If Pathfinder is part of the team, have him use the beacon to find the next circle location so you can try and predict where other teams will be coming from / going to. If not, head toward the bridges which lie in the center of the map; this will help you place yourself for the next zone.

THE AIR BASE

Also on the edge of the map, the Air Base offers a bunch of looting options, and hiding places. With 3 supply bins on each pier and open airships in front of each pier, there is always enough loot for a firefight. CAUTION – When landing here it IS possible to fall or drop a team member off the map.

Besides the supply bins and all the places to hide in a firefight, there are also some very well placed zip lines, perfect for getting you into or out of the action. They are also a great tool for third partying someone engaged in battle.

If you are playing and NOT the jumpmaster your primary offensive role will be to support them wherever they choose to land. You can use the ping system to recommend any of those places (see more about the ping system later). Be aware any location can turn into an offensive location.

THE LOOT. STRATEGICALLY LOOTING FOR OFFENSIVE PLAY.

One of the most fun parts of Apex Legends is looting. Finding those orange and white supply bins of happiness is always exciting. Knowing what to take can be a bit more daunting as the amount of things you can carry is limited until you find a backpack. Initially, grab anything you can get your paws on, especially if you have chosen to make a hot drop (lots of other teams fighting for the same items). If you are shooting for a truly offensive match, your primary loot concerns should be:

WEAPONS: A dream sheet of offensive weapons for the long range fighter would be a Longbow DMR and a G7 Scout. If you'd rather be up in everyone's face spraying bullets with gleeful abandon go for the Alternator SMG and Peacekeeper Shotgun. Now, obviously ANY of these weapons can be used offensively, however if faced with a lot of options these work very well together.

Don't be mistaken – in an immediate drop something as simple as an RE-45 pistol will quickly knock an enemy with less than two full magazines, if they have no shield. When you have first landed ANY weapon can be a good weapon.

Throwables (the handy frag grenade, a shield destroying arc star that will disorient the enemy causing their screen to fuzz, or a well placed thermite grenade – if thrown in a room this will create a wall that will provide constant damage to the enemy allowing you to devise your next moves) are as much of an offensive threat as they are a defensive ploy.

AMMO: Grab as much as you can! You can never have enough ammo. Also, since it may take some time for you to find your personal favorite combination of weapons, you may want to have a couple different types of ammo on hand in the case that you want to switch. Your team will also appreciate you if you are able to hook them up if they run out.

THE BACKPACK: Get one. The bigger the better, so upgrade it as much as possible. This way you can arm yourself with as many heals, armor shields, attachments and throwables as possible. If you are going to be playing aggressively you need to make sure you don't run out of these items and restock whenever you can.

ATTACHMENTS: It's hard to say what the best offensive attachment to have is. Magazines, stocks, and sights are great, but to become the best offensive player you have to work with what you have to get those kills.

SIGHTS/SCOPES: The closer you can see your enemy, the easier it is to land that headshot. The type of weapon you have will determine the best type of sight. There is no sense in putting a long range sight on a short range weapon, and one of the best things about this game is that it won't LET you do that. Some of the best sights offensively are the digital threat sights (Legendary)– these sights contain not only zoom magnification but also highlight enemies in red.

Magazine capacity plays a critical role in offensive firefights; therefore having as much ammo as possible in your weapon gives you the advantage in battle. Every gun comes with the ability to upgrade the magazine size up to three times, depending on the weapon the capacity will be different. By the time you reach the third tier of magazine (purple magazine) you should have more than enough ammo to take down any opponent if all your shots land on that enemy. More ammo means less time loading, more firepower, more bullets whizzing at the enemy; even if your aim is off, if you can spray a ton of bullets you stand a better chance of hitting someone.

HEALTH AND ARMOR: You obviously can't become a Champion of the Arena if you die. Health and armor are no brainers here. A great thing about Apex is that the game will alert you if you are going to choose an item that is less quality than what you currently have equipped, and not allow you to pick it up, so you won't accidentally drop Legendary armor for normal armor – know that if your armor has no shield left it will swap out for any other armor with shield. This is why the shield cells and batteries are so important.

Health is a standard need for any shooter, and Apex gives you two different sizes of health kits. There are also the previously mentioned shield cells and shield batteries which fix damaged armor. Unless you have dead eye aim, plan on carrying a lot of both if you are going offensive; lots of firefights = lots of damage for everyone.

Keep an eye open for triangular shaped Apex packs - glowing (totally technical term here) robots on small tripods; shoot these and pop them open for some good gear. They aren't always easy to spot but worth the find. Keep in mind they will make noise, which will reveal their location. Remember, they will also make noise when you shoot them, revealing YOUR location. If you are having trouble locating the source of the noise look high. Many times they are found on the very top of buildings. If you are in a room look in corners or under stairs for anything glowing or beeping.

THE ENVIRONMENT. ZIP LINES, BALLOONS, AND CARE PACKAGES.

A truly offensive player will use all aspects of their environment, in typical and sometimes crazy ways. Apex Legends offers a boatload of ways, both typical and a bit crazy. All you need is a little creativity, some skill, a dash of luck, and the drive to become…. A CHAMPION OF THE ARENA.

USING THE ENVIRONMENT FOR OFFENSIVE PLAY.

ZIP LINES: The zip lines that are found in Apex can be some of your biggest allies in your quest for domination. If used well, they can allow for great advantages in firefights. You can use the zip lines to quickly travel to enemy locations, or to get a drop on unsuspecting enemies. If you are a more advanced player you can even get kills while moving along the lines, and while enemies travel them as well.

Getting kills from or on the zip lines require a steady aim and a bit of luck, but it can happen more than you might think. While found all over the map, the best zip line systems are in Relay and Swamps.

BALLOONS: Balloons can also be used to get a drop on the enemy, but at a much faster rate than the zip lines. You can reach the highest points of the map by using the balloons, but beware of landing outside of the play zone. If you are caught in a firefight as the circle closes in, balloons will give you an offensive edge to fight longer, getting in some last second kills before you have to use them to flee the area.

Also just like the zip lines, you can shoot people traveling on the balloons; if you are in the closing circle scenario, use the environment around you (banners, rocks, buildings) as cover and stage an attack on any team leaving the area to run from the circle or simply go to another area to find loot.

On top of that, you can travel from one balloon to another to get the jump on the best loot and the best spots to stalk your prey.

SUPPLY DROPS: Literally love dropped from the sky. Just as literally? A death marker. The supply drops, while offering some fantastic offensive gear (guns, attachments, etc), are like a beacon to other players hoping to score some easy kills or better supplies. Everyone on the map will know the location of the supply drop, announced by a blue beacon pulsing in the sky.

Supply drops arguably contain the most powerful weapons in the game, however keep in mind they offer limited and unrefillable ammo. Stand watch in a secluded space; these crates are guaranteed to have at least one or two other offensive strikers headed to them for those elusive legendary weapons. If your placement is good enough you can easily pick off teams as they race for the prize.

If you choose to approach these the other way around, and decide to go for the loot, you better move fast. Octane would be a great choice for supply drop raids. His speed is paralleled to no other. Also, Gibralter, who is primarily a more defensive player, would be a great offensive asset here; he could drop a shield around the team to protect them as you race for the drop.

THE PING SYSTEM, AN OFFENSIVE TOOL NEVER TO BE FORGOTTEN. Saving the best and most unique aspect of this Battle Royale, the ping system is invaluable in offensive action. This system is a never before done way of communicating with your team negating the use of a microphone. By either double tapping or long pressing a button you can bring up a radial menu to communicate with your team members in a variety of ways. The most beneficial of these ways to offense would be the ability to double tap on an enemy revealing the location and distance of an enemy to your team in real time. This can allow for aggressors to devise tactics to eliminate the other players such as direct attacks, gaining height advantage to shoot down, flanking to surround, or drawing fire in a certain direction to push them in a different direction.

The ping system can identify objects in the field such as better gear or weapons for your teammates who may not have had to opportunity to find them yet, making you a more tactically well rounded and dangerous team.

The last offensive feature of the ping system is to mark a location to direct your team to a new position. All of these things, if used in conjunction with a microphone, will make your team a serious offensive threat.

Tactics are a huge beast to tackle. Entire books could be written on this subject, so the goal of this short breakdown of the best and most vital offensive tactics for Apex Legends will help you learn to be stronger, faster, and better. Hopefully these tips will help you become one of the top offensive players, but know that it will take many hours of practice, play, and loss to develop a foolproof plan to consistently claim victory in the Arena. ∎

DEFENSIVE TACTICS

Just like offensive tactics, defensive tactics are present in every game, whether you are aware of them or not. If you are a newer player to the game, these defensive tricks will really help your game. And remember – you don't have to confine yourself to playing only offensively or defensively – take what you need from this chapter and leave the rest.

There are tons of ways to amp your defensive tactics. From choosing your character to knowing how to use the terrain to your advantage, defensive play isn't just about how many other players you can kill quickly, it's about survival. Sometimes that can mean very few kills and making it to the top 3; sometimes that can mean skulking around for the fun of it and seeing how long you can survive without killing anyone!

A note on Camping (**from the Urban Dictionary**):
A term used most frequently in first-person shooter video games, "camping" refers to the act of hiding or otherwise remaining in a hidden, obscured, or safe location in order to ambush an enemy or objective, or to avoid harm.

There is much controversy over whether or not camping is a respectable strategy; some claim camping is cowardly and cheap, while others maintain that it is intelligent and strategic. *"There's a guy camping outside the door with a Covenant Energy Sword. Be careful, lest he perpetrate the ownage against you."*

"That sniper-@# sniper be camping on top of the base."*

by ghostpigeon July 25, 2005) we will not teach you how to hide. Muahahahahahahaha.

BACK AT THE BEGINNING.

In offensive tactics, we talked about certain characters that are a more natural fit for an aggressive campaign. Now we are going to talk about the other characters that are more suited for protecting the wild ones in the group. And, touch on Wraith and Mirage, the two players that aren't particularly offensive or defensive.

YOUR DEFENSIVE HEROES ARE:

THE ORIGINALS

- **LIFELINE** (Combat Medic)
  "Bleed, patch, and keep moving."
- **GIBRALTAR** (Shielded Fortress)
  "Try and move me."
- **PATHFINDER** (Forward Scout)
  "Remember me friends."

THE UNLOCKABLE:

- **CAUSTIC** (Toxic Trapper)
  "Join my experiment below."

THE PLAYERS
LIFELINE

The ultimate defensive champion found in the arena, Lifeline is an extremely valuable asset in the game and, at the time of writing, is one of the most popular characters in this title (so popular in fact, a certain other Battle Royale has a new character skin that looks suspiciously like her). She is a very easy character to use, and as team medic, offers a lot of tools that will help both her and the others recover and push forward to become the ultimate champion team. Not only can she heal, revive, and shield, she can call in defensive care packages. Lifeline has medium speed and agility.

Lifeline's passive ability is Combat Medic. With this she can revive a knocked teammate faster, while protected by a shield wall (be aware of where you aim the shield). Any healing items used are 25% faster.

Her Tactical ability is called D.O.C. (Drone of Compassion) Heal Drone. This compassionate (and somewhat adorable) drone automatically heals those near it over a short period of time. This is a super handy defensive tool as it allows Lifeline to heal her team after they have taken damage. If you aren't as strong in a firefight, you are still able to contribute to the team in an invaluable way.

Her ultimate ability is Care Package. Calling it in with a perky quip, Lifeline is able to bring in a personal care package, with 3 premium defensive items, typically consisting of armor, a knockdown shield, and a phoenix kit (or some similar combination). Even if you are offensively weak, your team will greatly appreciate Lifeline. Ultimate accelerants (a consumable that can be looted) is especially useful with given to / taken by Lifeline as it revs up her ultimate to fill faster.

GIBRALTAR

If you have ever dreamed of being a walking, talking tank, Gibraltar is your man. Being big and bulky makes Gibraltar a force that requires a bit of patience to play. Although he has the slowest speed and most limited agility of the group, Gibraltar is like a moving wall. He is a human defensive weapon, packing shields and mortar strikes to provide your team with a large amount of security to push through the more dangerous firefights.

His passive ability is called Gun Shield. Aiming down sights deploys a gun shield that will block enemy fire. If you crouch while aiming, he protects almost his entire body. Especially valuable if you are being attacked by a hidden party, this will buy extra seconds of defense while Gibraltar seeks out the offense.

His tactical ability is called Dome of Protection. This will drop a dome shield that will block all attacks for 15 seconds. If the team acts as one they will be able to move together under this shield to get to a place safer for defending their position. This could mean fleeing the area, gaining cover in a building, or using an ability of a different character to move quickly (i.e. Wraith's portals). An important thing to note about this ability is that it will also block outgoing shots; if your team wants to fire on the enemy they will need to be outside of this shield.

Gibraltar's ultimate ability is called Defensive Bombardment. He can call in a concentrated mortar strike on any position you mark with smoke. Be aware that this attack, like Bangalore's air strike, will damage anything in its circle, including teammates.

PATHFINDER

Offering a virtually unending stream of positivity, Pathfinder may be the most cheerful of your Apex options (although Lifeline comes a close second). Always ready to offer helpful advice, Pathfinder is like a robotic swiss army knife, coming equipped with hooks and grapples that allow him and his team to quickly get around the map and get to the harder to reach areas of the map.

Even though his speed and agility fall in the middle of the pack, Pathfinders grappling hook will give you a bit of extra pep in your step when you need to move more quickly.

His passive ability is Insider Knowledge. Pathfinder will scan a survey beacon to see the next ring location. This is extremely important for a team to be on the defensive, allowing them the jump to get to the best areas in the new zone before their competitors.

Pathfinder's tactical ability, Grappling Hook, will get you into hard to impossible to reach spaces, getting you to prime loot or out of dangerous firefights. In an extreme situation, Pathfinder can use the hook to pull enemies closer. If he has a SMG or shotgun now would be the time to use it to impact maximum damage on the enemy.

Finally, the ultimate ability, the Zip Line Gun. It's important to remember if you are defending yourselves, that the Zip Line Gun can be used by anyone once it's placed. Having talked about zip line benefits in the offensive section, you should already be familiar with the versatility of this tool. In a sticky firefight where defensive is the only option left, his Zip Line Gun is the Hail Mary pass to safety. Use it to gain distance or get across ravines quickly.

CAUSTIC

One of the two original unlockables, Caustic has a very… well…. Caustic personality. He is a dual threat on the battlefield, with his abilities to block the paths of other players and literally jamb entryways so other enemies get trapped. This can be good either defensively, to allow time to flee a congested area or offensively, to pin the enemy in place and make it easier to pick them off.

Caustic is one of the slower and less agile players you can choose, but his Nox Gas ability will allow him to gain the tactical advantage he needs to deflect enemies.

His passive: Nox Vision. Nox Vision gives Caustic threat vision on enemies moving through his gas. This is vital for defense against multiple enemies in contained firefights. With the ability to be the only person able to see through the gas, Caustic is given an incredible defensive ability, and using the ping system, is able to share his vision with the team.

His tactical ability, Nox Gas Trap, will place up to 6 canisters that release deadly nox gas when shot or triggered by the movement of enemies. This gas slows and disorients all enemies (while taking a minor amount of life) that are in its vicinity, allowing time to move to a safer location, or reposition yourselves to shoot the enemy. It's great to throw this if you need to revive a team member as it will hide you from view and keep others from charging your position. It is important to know that these traps can be disarmed by shooting the colored area on the bottom of the canisters. If the correct spot is hit, the trap will disarm and retract.

The ultimate ability for Caustic is the Nox Gas Grenade. This will blanket a large area in nox gas, making retreat the only option.

THE WILDCARDS: WRAITH AND MIRAGE.

We mentioned before that the original character Wraith, and the other unlockable character, Mirage are both adept characters that can play either offensive or defensive. Here is a breakdown of both; hopefully it will help you decide which way you will prefer to use the characters!

WRAITH

As an interdimensional skirmisher, Wraith is able to use voids to her offensive and defensive advantage. While not a character to be taken lightly, she is better suited for the more cunning and less brute force inclined players, if you want to maximize her duality. She can avoid gunfire by running into the void or use her portals to jump others to certain spots of the arena - either to save them from massacre or drop them in an advantageous spot to massacre others. Wraith is a very tortured character, being destroyed by the very gifts that save her.

She is able to manipulate her movement and virtually disappear during a firefight. The key to learning Wraith is deciding how you want to use the abilities; be it for offense, defense, or all out confusion. She is one of the top 3 chosen characters of the original roster and is not likely to lose that popularity due to her duplicity.

The passive ability: Voices from the Void. A voice will come from, you guessed it, the void and warn when danger approaches, making it a very useful defensive skill. It will also warn when someone is aiming at you. It seems to be on your side…

The tactical ability: Into the Void, allows Wraith to reposition herself quickly, through the safety of the "void space". She may still be visible to other players, but cannot take damage during this short amount of time. It is up to you to decide if you want to use this as an offensive or defensive tool, but it is a good idea to try both.

Finally her ultimate ability: Dimensional Rifts. Wraith can lay a portal in two different locations to create a shortcut for herself and her team. The distance from one to another is limited, as is the portal time of 60 seconds. Like Pathfinders zip lines and grapples, once these portals are placed anyone, including the enemy can use them, so be cautious in placing them.

MIRAGE

If you had to sum up Mirage in three words flashy, confident, and cunning (in a very ditzy way) would put him together nicely. With the ability to cloak himself in invisibility, while setting decoys and flitting about a bit faster than normal. It's very doable to use Mirage in either offensive or defensive modes, and he is easily one of the top two defensive players in the game. He is also unique because he can use an ability to send out two decoys while dropping at the beginning of the game.

...and for his first trick. Encore is Mirage's passive ability. This passive will automatically drop a decoy cloak for 5 seconds every time Mirage is knocked, hopefully throwing off the fighter that knocked him, allowing him to get to safety, and / or a teammate to knock the bamboozled player that thinks they knocked Mirage. Whoa. He gets confusing.

Mirage's tactical ability is the Psyche Out. After pointing the direction he wants it to go, Mirage unleashes a decoy to confuse the enemy. The decoy will run in the direction pointed, so be aware of terrain obstacles that may stop the decoy's movement before you want it to. This is so great for defense since it can catch other players (especially the nervous one) off guard, causing those trying to be sneaky snakes to reveal their locations prematurely, giving your team a jump on defending themselves.

Mirage's ultimate ability is called Vanishing Act. As the ability suggests, Mirage just vanishes. But, showman that he is, Mirage can't simply VANISH. He instead spawns a small horde of decoys and THEN vanishes. The chaos this can cause can make it easier offensively for a teammate to sneak up on the enemy, or defensively for Mirage's team to move to ground safer and better suited for getting an advantage on the offending enemy.

USING THE MAP DEFENSIVELY.

In the offensive tactics section, we talked about the best places to drop for loot, and hot drops. There really is no "safe" spot to drop defensively; the only sure thing here is to try and avoid prime loot locations if you want to play a more relaxed game. Since we're focusing on the defensive in this part, let's focus on the amazing terrain of Apex Legends and all the hidden gifts it offers.

THE TERRAIN/ ENVIRONMENT

They can be some of the most compelling and magical aspects of game play. But, it's also a vital tool that can be used to your advantage in winning battles, eluding enemies, devising elaborate flanking maneuvers, or just camping out until unsuspecting prey falls across your path. In Apex Legends, the map offers a myriad of terrain types to hone your skills to become the Champions of the Arena.

TERRAIN AND ENVIRONMENT TIPS: SCENARIO 1 BUILDINGS, CARS, AND DOWNHILL SLOPES

The shot above is to portray everything going on immediately in front of you. The ring is closing; if you were on the edge of the circle (with the edge to your back) you can assume all the main action will take place from the front; right or left. Knowing this; you will want to survey the terrain and environment to maximize your advantage.

A FEW OF YOUR OPTIONS INCLUDE:

Running forward and crouching by the tree to regroup: check inventory; drop unnecessary items; plan your next move.

Investigate the building immediately to your left for potential loot.

If you are in an encounter with another group your options are great; there are multiple environmental aspects you can use to provide defensive barriers, including a building, vehicles, the trees, and a balloon.

To use the vehicles defensively, stand behind them, move from one to another to gain better views, or jump on top to gain height advantage.

The building: go inside; this will prevent special attacks and regular guns from direct damage infliction. If you are playing a certain character (i.e. Caustic), you can use your gas traps to literally block the door from entry by opponents (providing they don't know how to kick down or disable the trap). Many buildings offer multiple levels, providing numerous hiding, crouching, climbing, and virtually camouflaged areas to remain hidden or provide cover from the enemy.

Downhill slopes and mud terrains can be used to move rapidly; your character will not stop sliding until it either collides with an object or reaches the end of the slope. Also, while sliding, almost all of your weapons, gadgets, and specials are still available for use, providing a combination of movement and attack abilities. As you move at a faster pace while sliding then running, this tactic is extremely valuable in evading those seeking to take you out of the arena.

TERRAIN AND ENVIRONMENT TIPS SCENARIO 2: ZIP LINES, MOUNTAINS/ RIDGES, AND BANNERS

There are so many unique and sometimes underused environmental additions in Apex Legends.

Zip lines can be used in a multitude of ways. To get from building to building, as a rapid way to get into the zone, as a defensive maneuver to evade enemy fire or escape battle altogether, as an attack to pounce down on unsuspecting enemies. A beautiful thing about zip lines is your ability to get on or off them at any point, and change direction at any time. This makes the zip lines a supremely versatile tool in game play and strategy.

BANNERS. While not as commonly used, banners provide a great way to deflect enemy gunfire, keep your champion hidden (assuming they don't shoot your feet), and are a visual distraction if you are standing directly in front of them. As the banners change to show new kill leaders / teams, depending on your character and outfit, you can literally blend into the image shown on the banner. Banners are probably the least used and most commonly forgotten pieces of the environment, yet they appear in every game at the same places ready to offer an environmental advantage.

MOUNTAINS/RIDGES. Some of the most difficult places on the map to reach, mountains and ridges can also be some of the most rewarding if you are able to reach them. They require skill and practice mixed with luck to attain peak position. However, once atop them, the ability to see so much map at once provides unimaginable advantage to you and your team.

DEATH BOXES. So vital for defense, the death boxes (dropped by downed players) are vital the further into the game you go. When everything is looted and picked over, the boxes offer a great option to restock; getting better armor, more ammo, different attachments and shields. These boxes will also glow different colors indicating epic or legendary loot.

RESPAWN. Like the ping system we talked about in the offensive section, the respawn feature is another very unique aspect pioneered by Apex. This is a feature that has gained immense popularity in other Battle Royales because of the wild success it has had in Apex Legends.

One of the greatest defensive features of the Apex terrain, the respawn beacons are scattered across the map, marked by a glowing green symbol. When a teammate is downed, you can collect his banner and deliver it to a beacon, causing that player to be respawned on a respawn ship and makes them able to rejoin the game. Another great feature of the respawn beacons? They are usually located near supply bins, which, if they haven't been looted yet, will help gear up the newly revived player(s). A perfect way to use the ping system and respawn beacon is for the downed player/players to "ping" the location of their banner first, then "ping" again once you have picked them up. This second ping will bring up the nearest respawn beacon to you with the distance marked so you have an easier time finding it to bring them back to the game as soon as possible. There are no limits on how often you can respawn a team member, other than the closing ring and narrowing of the map. Once the circle is small it's hard to wait for the banners to load into the respawn beacon.

LEVELING GUIDE

While leveling in Apex can be daunting because of the grind, we show you how it can actually be more fun than you might realize. Like many popular games, Apex relies on a leveling system that encourages you to play and to complete specific tasks along the way. Play more, complete more tasks, even log-in regularly, and you'll level up steadily as a result. You even get rewards for leveling up, making this a great incentive to keep pushing toward higher levels with your characters.

Apex features a level cap, giving you a lofty goal to work towards from the get-go. Right now, the cap is set at 110, which will take the typical player many months to reach.

Work harder and you'll level faster as a result! It's unclear whether Apex plans on adding more levels in the future, but it's quite possible the level cap might increase with a future expansion patch. Most players are still trying to reach the current level cap and that's likely why you're reading this section.

Learn more hint, tips, and tactics for leveling; how to do so faster; and what types of rewards you get for moving up the ladder. It's good to know what you can expect for spending hours to advance one level, so we dish the details below.

If you haven't dropped into Kings Canyon for a match yet, it's a good time to hop into a game and get started! After playing a few matches you'll start to understand what you can expect from the game and how much fun and excitement there is available to you in a variety of ways. Every player can enjoy the game the way that they want, whether they are trying to level, customize their character, or find cool weapons and items.

LEVELING UP REWARDS

When you level up in the game, you get rewarded for doing so. You can earn two different types of rewards: Legend Tokens or Apex Packs.

Every time you level up to the next level in the beginning, level 21 and lower, you get an Apex Pack. Once you reach level 21, you only get a Pack every other level. You can only earn up to 45 free Apex Packs total when leveling up, as you push to the top level.

In addition to the Packs, you also get Legend Tokens. These Tokens can be earned all the way up to level 110. There is no cap on the number of Tokens that you can earn or receive in the game, so even if you make it to level 110, you can keep earning and stashing Tokens for some exciting item purchases.

Legend Tokens can be used to purchase items in the game, such as skins, quips, banners, and more. These free items are also handed out at random in the game. You might be able to snag a few without spending any of your Tokens at all just by playing enough matches. These free items are given out at random quality levels, so you could end up getting a Legendary item for free if you're lucky enough!

Along with items, crafting metals are also given out randomly to players as well. These powerful materials are used to create killer new weapons and to improve the look of your character. You can also purchase a recolored skin from the store using metals if you have enough of them saved up. Almost every skin in the game can be crafted, as long as they are not ultra-rare Heirloom items. These items are only found inside Packs.

Legend Tokens can also be used to buy other Legends in the game that don't unlock when you start playing. Caustic and Mirage are just two of the cool characters that must be purchased before you can use them, and Apex Legends promises the release of many additional Legends in the future as well.

Players that work hard to reach higher levels will be rewarded handsomely with Packs, Legend Tokens, and free items, which are three good reasons that underscore why it's so valuable to try and level your character.

GAINING XP

Each time you go into a game and play you'll have various opportunities to gain experience. Different actions earn different amounts of experience, so take the time to learn what you can do to unlock the biggest XP boosts as you play.

Check out our simple charts below and learn how much experience you can gain from assorted Combat, Survival, and Team-related actions that you complete while playing Apex Legends.

COMBAT
- Kill - +50 XP
- Kill Leader - +50 XP
- First Kill of the Day - +500 XP
- Champion Kill - +500 XP

SURVIVAL
- Survival Time – +3 XP per second
  (180 XP per minute survived in the game)
- Win – +900 XP
- Top 3 – +300 XP
- Match Victory - +500 XP

TEAM
- Revive Ally – +25 XP
- Respawn Ally – +200 XP
- Play with Champion – +500 XP
- Play with Friends – +5% Survival Time XP per Friend

These are not the only things you can gain experience from. There are plenty of other activities that will offer you experience points as well when you complete them. The list above just includes the normal everyday activities that help you accumulate experience, so always watch for new events and activities that you can use to earn even more.

The general rule of thumb here is that if you play well, you will be able to gain more XP. So learning how to play Apex Legends better, and more efficiently, will help you advance to higher levels more quickly. Gaining enough experience to reach the next level in Apex Legends starts off pretty easy but s-l-o-w-l-y becomes more difficult as you progress. Moving up a level is always an achievement worth celebrating as you play Apex Legends, so get out there, start playing, and work your way up to the top level while unlocking some exciting loot along the way!

HOW TO MAXIMIZE YOUR XP HAUL

Learning to maximize your XP earnings will help you level more quickly and reliably, which is perfect if you're the type of player that wants to unlock more loot in less time. Keep reading to learn what activities you should focus on to help you level-up your character. Some say that grinding (slow and steady playing) is the best way to gain levels, while others take a more strategic approach to leveling up. Learn the different leveling techniques used by top-level players and decide how you want to level your own characters.

*** Focus on survival and avoid any sort of combat in order to maximize your XP gains to the highest extent.

The XP awards are mostly dedicated to motivate players to actually log into the game, play it, not die, and do their part for their team.

The time you spend in the game is going to give you more experience than how well you are doing in the game overall. Your performance may not necessarily provide the return on investment that you might think. This is why **it is best to focus on survival.** Living with just a couple kills is more useful for leveling than dying quickly after getting several kills.

Staying alive rewards you with a continuous stream of XP in Apex Legends, but getting kills is another way to unlock rewards. That said, kills only offer small XP boosts, so kills should never be the goal over staying alive, or you'll lose out on a large amount of XP as a result.

Example: If you stay alive in the game for at least 5 minutes, it is the same XP points as getting 18 kills. This is a serious amount of XP for not doing much of anything.

By fighting enemies and generally just working with your team, you'll acquire additional XP rewards. Reviving teammates isn't just helpful for your team's survival, it gives you with a small amount of XP as well, just like making kills and fighting off attacking enemies. Try to balance performance and survival in your game for the absolute best rate of XP gains.

Example: Landing in 1st Place accounts for 15% of your XP, especially if you're playing in a team with friends instead of randomly matching with someone. Your survival time comprises nearly 75% of your XP in the game; combat is roughly 9% of the XP that you can gain in the game, while team support such as reviving takes up roughly 1%.

If you're trying to level up as efficiently as possible, purchasing the Battle Pass is a simple way to speed-up the process. The Battle Pass helps players level-up faster, and unlocks additional XP bonuses that free players don't have access to.

HOW MUCH XP DO YOU NEED?

Now that you've begun playing Apex Legends and you're raking in some nice XP each match, it's time to focus on just how much XP is needed to reach the top levels in the game. The amount of XP goes up with each level, making leveling early on much easier than it is later in the game. Looking at the bar at the top of the screen informs you how much XP you need to reach your next level. The table below explains how the levels in Apex Legends work.

One Level Requires 29,500 XP

Level 1 – 100 Require 2,920,500

Level 1 – 110 Requires 3,215,500

To Reach Level 110, You Need 35,000 XP Per Day

TIPS FOR LEVELING FASTER

There are many ways to accelerate your leveling now that you understand how the XP points work and how you can amass them. When it comes to playing inside the game, focusing on survival, then combat and team-play as a secondary goal, will help you earn experience more reliably and level-up faster.

Play with your friends! The more you play with your friends, the more experience you're going to get. This is because you can net up to 5% survival time bonuses and an extra 300 XP if you finish in the top three spots of the game.

Don't have friends on your console to team up with and play with? No worries, you can make friends in the game when you want to gain maximum XP by playing with them!

You can join the Apex Legends Discord and check out the Team Recruitment section, which brings together players that want friends to play with to gain more XP in the game. The Apex Legends Forum is also a great place to meet people and get together to form friendships and alliances.

Stay away from combat until the end of the game. This is easier said than done, but when you are trying to make it to the top three you have to avoid taking damage as much as possible. Lay low and let the other squads take each other out, leaving your team with as few opponents as possible to conquer at the end of the game.

Look for a champion in the group. If you can take out the champion in the game, regardless of who they are with, unless they are in your team, you can grab yourself 500 XP which is a big deal and a good way to level up your character faster.

Be a sniper. If you sit up high and take out other players in the game, you can grab extra XP for every kill you make. If you can do this and stay alive in the game until the end, the amount of extra XP really adds up.

Know which person is the leader! Claim bonus XP when you kill the leader of any group you're fighting against.

Try to emerge as the victor. It is crucial to stay alive and in the game as long as possible. Surviving until the end is how the most XP points are gained.

Use the XP modifiers if you have the Battle Pass. This helps boost your levels much quicker. Plus, boosters stack, which means they give you multiple increased XP gains. Additionally, the Battle Pass drops a weekly bonus of up to 25,000 XP for every Legend that you have. If you have this maxed-out on one Legend, you can change that Legend and gain the points on another.

Additional XP with a daily kill bonus. There is not only 500 XP that is given for your first kill of the game, but you also get 500 XP for your first kill every day thereafter with every Legend that you play with. Use a different Legend with each match to unlock that daily 500 XP bonus for all of them.

Be the champion in the game. The champion in the game nabs you even more XP every day that you hold that title. This means you can grab 500 XP just for being the champion and signing-on to play.

Be cautious during your time in the game. By laying low, making the most of your cover and surroundings, and generally not taking initiatives at the start, you're essentially maximizing your XP gains.

Find the right balance. It is important that you maintain a balance between notching kills, wins, being a team player, and grinding in general. With this approach, you can gain as much XP as possible but also maximize your enjoyment.

Switch between characters. When you switch between characters in the game, you can max out the XP points available since you get bonus XP for each character that you play. The amount of XP you gain is then added to your profile, regardless of the character you are using.

Just keep in mind that you cannot level all of your characters at once, they have to be handled individually. Spending a ton of time on one character is not going to help level your other characters.

Focus on survival. Many players like to rush into combat as soon as possible and they often die early on in matches because of that. Take a more defensive approach and focus on surviving over killing other players and you'll automatically begin earning more XP per match as a result.

So, how long will it take you to actually level up to the highest level?

Even with the Battle Pass in your hands, you can expect to spend around 100 or more hours to reach the highest tiers of Apex Legends. Those that do not have the Battle Pass may find themselves putting in an extra 50 or so hours on top of the 100 hours. Though that is a lot of time, the hours required to advance in subsequent seasons has dropped.

Once you hit the highest level, you get a pretty awesome animated badge to show off. The bling makes a nice addition to your homepage, and lets others know you are a legitimately seasoned player.

By going into the game with a focus on having fun and surviving, you'll start accumulating more experience with each round that you play. Have fun, be smart, play hard, and become a reliable teammate that others want to play with!

BATTLE PASS BASICS AND BUNDLES

Just like other battle royale games, Apex Legends offers you the chance to make the most out of your playing time with tons of extras and upgrades.

The Battle Pass is one of the most well-known ways to accomplish this, and we break down the info to educate you on what you can expect with this type of pass.

Most importantly, the more you play and level-up in the game with the Battle Pass activated, the faster your progress will go and more rewards you can get—just like Fortnite's!

In Apex, you have the option to purchase just the Battle Pass or the Battle Pass Bundle.

HOW DOES THE BATTLE PASS WORK?

You sign-up and pay for a Battle Pass, and start playing. The more you play, the more rewards you're able to collect. You can even jump right into the arena and start making gains! With each level you gain, a new level on the Battle Pass will be added. This then unlocks exclusive rewards for you to use in the game.

The Battle Pass is a great addition to have while you're playing the game because you get a lot of extras for having it. If you do not have the pass and you level up, you do not gain as much in return. Sure, you get some stuff playing without the pass, but it's not nearly as cool!

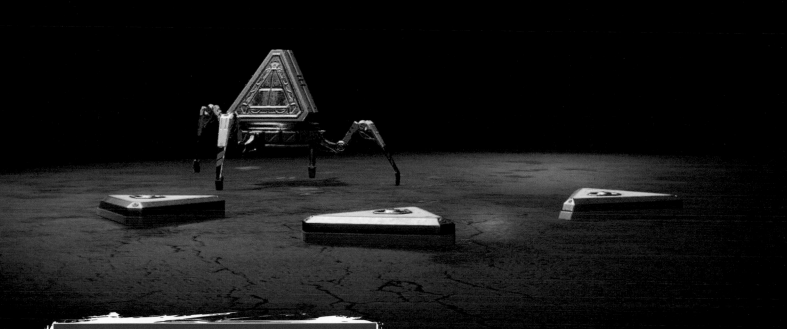

You only have to play for around an hour a day to unlock most of the goodies. They include skins, bling, parachutes, virtual currency, emotes and dances, and more.

Also good news, you don't have to grind away countless hours to get them. You can also purchase each of the tiers that you don't make for $1.50 or 150 Apex Coins to get to that level. If you don't unlock that level, then you won't get all of the free stuff that is added to the Battle Pass for that season.

You pay $9.50 or 950 Apex Coins to unlock the Pass.

Once you decide to commit the time to playing the game—and getting good at it—you might as well get the pumped-up bonuses that come with the Battle Pass every single time you play.

BATTLE PASS

The original Battle Pass comes with 100 tiers of unlockable content that is exclusive to just the Battle Pass holders, and not those that are just in the game.

BATTLE PASS BUNDLE

The Bundle comes with everything that is offered in the Battle Pass, plus a way to unlock 25 levels without having to level them on your own. This instantly gives you the levels you need to get the rewards you want.

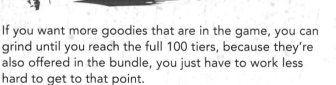

If you want more goodies that are in the game, you can grind until you reach the full 100 tiers, because they're also offered in the bundle, you just have to work less hard to get to that point.

You pay $28 or 2,800 Apex Coins to unlock the Pass.

APEX LEGENDS LEGEND BONUS

If you want to move faster through the levels and gain extra points while leveling up, then taking advantage of the Apex Legends Legend Bonus is the way to go. This is a booster for those that want to get to a higher level without having to put in all that grinding time, day after day.

When you select this bonus, you can get up to 25,000 extra Battle Pass points. You just need to find out how much your in-match survival time is each week for each character and you can get the bonus for each of them. Hit the bonus with your main character and switch to get even more points on another one.

BATTLE PASS SKINS

There are numerous skins that can be purchased, gathered from loot crates, or even added to the rewards from the Battle Pass.

Every season brings out new skins and new Legends. You can even get some Battle Pass skins that aren't found anywhere else. You just need to level up to unlock them.

Season 1 is when Octane was introduced to the Legends map. He is high-flying fun and ensures that you have a great time. You have to purchase these characters as they do not come with the pass, but new characters are usually introduced with each new season.

BATTLE PASS REWARDS

There are many different rewards that you get for being a Battle Pass owner, which means you want to make sure you know exactly what can be obtained when you sign up for this pass.

You can also grab useful items when you have the pass. With everything from small med packs, to new loot, parachutes, and other themed items, you can find them all from the pass that offers additional rewards.

These rewards are worth a lot of Apex Coins when you have them because they are exclusive to those that have these passes or purchase loot boxes.

BATTLE PASS SEASONS

Just like with Fortnite, there are different Seasons that are introduced to players that sign up with the Battle Passes.

SEASON 1: MARCH

The current season is Season 1. It is the latest (and greatest) pass that was introduced to new players of the game. Launched in March 2019, this pack opened up a lot of new extras, skins, bonuses, and perks to those that signed up for the pass.

SEASON 2: JUNE

New Legends arrived in June, introduced with Season 2. This has undoubtedly changed the pace for those that already had a regular player or character currently. Cool new skins, bonuses, and other extra came with the arrival of Season 2.

SEASON 3: SEPTEMBER

Just like the other seasons, you can grab points that unlock bonuses, extras, skins, and more for you to play with inside the game. New weapons are also rumored to be introduced into the game for those that purchase the pass, giving those folks a first look at seeing and using these weapons in the game.

SEASON 4: DECEMBER

If you're the type that thrives on having the latest and greatest loot, then the Holiday-time drop of Season 4 is for you. EA will be providing skins, bonuses, extras, and more to those that are purchase the Battle Pass—making this occasion a great one to amass and hoard points for.

LOOT BOXES

If you want extra loot or free items, then spending a bit of money on loot boxes (that are almost like mystery bling bags) might be the best thing for you to do. This is also great if you like being surprised and appreciate the finger-tapping anticipation of wondering what is inside.

Loot boxes are broken down into packs. These come with three different items. They can be common, rare, or Legendary items inside the boxes. At least one of the items is going to be rare or better.

Players are expected to find an Epic item once in every four packs they purchase, evening out the odds. They should also get a Legendary item once in every 13 packs that they purchase. This is not a guarantee, though.

The loot boxes come with this type of loot inside them:
- Skins – These are for the Legends characters and also for weapons you have. They come in different themes and colors to choose from. Custom paint jobs, new outfits, and changes to looks help keep your character fresh and stylish.

- Banner Frames – This is the frame you see when a player dies or when it is on the load screen around the character. There are different images, patterns, colors, and more that can come with the frames.

- Banner Poses – This is also shown on the same screen, but the characters' poses are different when the frames are loading up.

- Stat Trackers – You can customize what is displayed on the banner in the game.

- Quips – Voice lines that can be common ones or more rarely spoken.

- Finishers – These are the signature finishing moves characters make when you use them in the game. These are all Legendary moves.

- Crafting Metals – You can find these in the game in smaller amounts. You need a lot to craft Legendary items, so gathering more always helps.

You also have a chance to get some of the rare heirloom item sets that are out there. The chances of this happening are slim, and while they are an exciting option to drool over, the odds of finding stuff like this is less than one percent.

Frankly, what you usually get in these packs are cosmetic tweaks. They are not going to help you get further in the game or make you stronger in any way. While visual upgrades are definitely nice to have and show off, they are not going to help you get better, which is definitely something to think about in your pursuit of them.

You can also get free boxes for leveling up. Every 100 levels will earn you a box, or you can purchase them on your own using Apex Coins.

HINTS AND TIPS

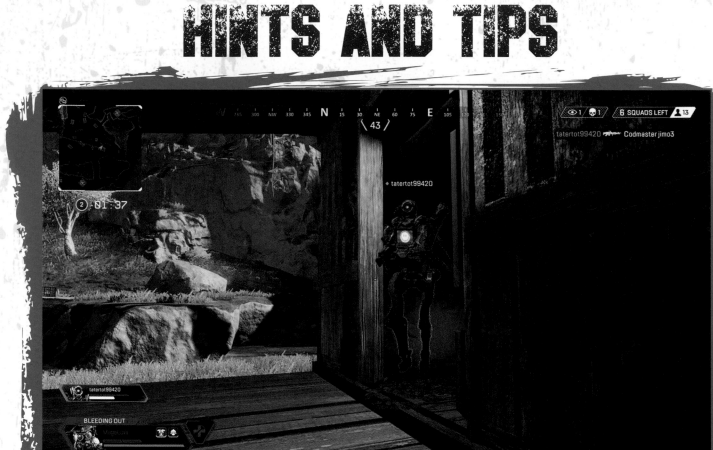

I f you want to dominate the arena, you need to learn the hints, tips, and tactics that give you an advantage. And ideally, it's not just you but also your teammates, who also know what to when things get heavy during gameplay. Apex Legends is about keeping your teammates alive, synchronizing, and making progress together.

The knowledge exists to give you an edge when making your way to becoming a top Legend. After rigorous testing and lots of inadvertent dying, here is our collection of the top tips and tactics for playing Apex Legends:

ALWAYS CHOOSE A PLAYER THAT MATCHES YOUR PLAYING STYLE

This should go without saying, but if a character is not easy or enjoyable for you to play or you're struggling, try another. The more aligned the character is to your style, sensibilities, and identity, the better you'll be as a player.

The character should also complement your squad, because you don't want a team of players with the same style. You want a diverse mix of competent and complementary players that mesh well together.

STAY CLOSE TO THE SQUAD YOU'RE WITH

Apex Legends is a game where teamwork and team awareness is critical. Since it is a squad-based game, staying close to your mates so you can bring players back, use each other's strengths, and more is the best way to survive and advance.

YOUR SQUAD

SMART KEYS DEFINITELY HELP

You can be much, much quicker if you use the smart or hot keys on the keyboard if you're playing on a PC. This is because you can easily attack, hold fire, or flee when the time comes. If you have to do a series of moves or clicks on your keyboard to do something, you might not be quick enough and it could cost you your life.

BE CAREFUL WHEN IT COMES TO THE REALLY GOOD STUFF

Of course, everyone wants to go after the best loot. Think of the Hunger Games, and how everything was piled up nicely. When you see something you want, pause and be smart about pursuing it. This means being aware of your surroundings, having backups, and making sure that the items are not just a trap to lure you in.

BECOME FAMILIAR WITH THE ARENA AND MAP AREA

Study your arena maps as much as possible. An awareness of your surroundings will not only help you find good loot faster, it will also enable you to escape sticky situations that inevitably occur in game.

USE ALL AVAILABLE FEATURES TO YOUR ADVANTAGE

When you have hot zones or jump towers around you, use 'em! If you're in a tight spot, they can definitely help you get out of a jam.

Practice using them before going into battle so it becomes second nature. Once you become proficient, you can even use the skill to take your enemies by surprise.

RESPAWN AND HELP YOUR SQUAD MATES

It is important that you respawn and help your teammates. When one of them is down, they might not be all the way out. This means that you can revive them, and they can continue the good fight with you.

If your teammates need a hand, pick them up, dust them off, and keep on playing!

INTERRUPT OTHER FIGHTS

If you happen on two other teams slugging it out, dive right in and take both out while they're depleted. If you hear the gunfire in the background during a game, run towards it and help the teams wipe each other out so your team continues to survive and thrive.

USE A NEW BODY SHIELD

Instead of recharging the body shield you're wearing, you can just discard and grab a new one. You might not have time to let the old one recharge. You can save more time by finding a new one, even if it is not the same color, because you're not whipping out those cells and batteries to charge up the one you have.

NO NEED TO FINISH OFF DOWNED ENEMIES RIGHT AWAY

If you are currently not the third team left in the battle, then there is no point in executing those players that are down and unable to defend themselves. Just let them be. If their team hasn't come back for them then they might not. You want to spend your time taking out the rest of the team that is still a threat to you.

YOU WILL BE FIGHTING MORE THAN ONE PERSON

When you engage in combat, know that you are not going to be fighting just one person. You will more than likely be engaged with at least three people. Even if you only see one, there are usually more lurking nearby.

GANG UP ON YOUR ENEMIES ONE-BY-ONE

One of the biggest mistakes teams make is when they matchup and fight enemies in one-on-one battles. Instead, your team should focus all of its energy on one foe at a time. This not only knocks them out faster but also lessens the individual damage you and your teammates have to absorb.

GRENADES ARE USEFUL

Flushing out and flustering enemies has never been easier with the use of grenades. You can slow-down their movement with the use of grenades or even stun them while they are trying to revive or heal while hiding behind something.

HOLSTER YOUR WEAPONS TO RUN FASTER

When you need to get out of a situation faster, holstering your weapons can actually make you move much faster than if you were carrying them around! You do this by holding down the swap weapons button, which tucks the weapon away temporarily.

DESTROY CAUSTIC'S GAS TRAPS

You can actually do this when you shoot at the base of the trap. Aim for the red part that is located below the black gas tank.

LAND ON THE OUTSKIRTS

If you're not the type that likes to land in the thick of the firefight, then consider landing on the outskirts of the map. There is loot here, you'll be much less visible, and won't have to worry about fighting someone right away.

WITH JUST A COUPLE OF GROUPS LEFT, DON'T RUSH

When you are fighting and there are only three or four groups left, no need to force the action. Be patient and wait for them to come and find you. This gives you the advantage of having to defend rather than attack, against a team that just survived other battles.

BE A MORE SLIPPERY TARGET

Of course always crouch down to avoid fire, but did you know you can also slide away by using the crouch option? You're a much harder target to hit if you're sliding down hills and whatnot.

SUPPLY BINS ARE AWESOME BUT HARD TO SPOT

These are harder to identify because they are usually pretty well hidden in most places. However, if you find them they are chock full of items, weapons, and extras for you to use.

They usually have some pretty high-end stuff in them too, mostly because they are hidden away much like the chests in Fortnite, but you gotta keep your eyeballs peeled to spot 'em.

LOOT TICKS, ON THE OTHER HAND, ARE IMPOSSIBLE TO MISS

There are things called loot ticks that shine pretty colors, emit lights into the sky, and make fun noises that you can hear when you get close enough to them. They always have a bit of loot inside so when you notice one, be sure to open!

LEARN HOW TO PING YOUR TEAMMATES

You want to make sure that everyone in your group is stocked-up with supplies when finding new loot. This means knowing how to ping them and let them know when you have found something. You just need to click on the items that you want to ping if you come across loot for everyone.

THERE IS NO DAMAGE FROM FALLS IN APEX LEGENDS

In most battle royale games, damage from falling from the sky or off high structures is most definitely something you have to worry about. In Apex, falling from any height does not harm you at all. There is literally no damage that comes from falling off a cliff or not using your glider to swoop down to your spot.

NO FALLING DAMAGE CAN BE WEAPONIZED

In fact, no falling damage can be a great advantage when you find yourself above players that you want to take out. Just jump down on top of them and you'll have the element of surprise.

MAKE SURE YOUR INVENTORY IS WELL MANAGED

Organization is usually not something most people want to bother with, but knowing where all your stuff is can come in handy when you're under duress. Organize, declutter, manage, and memorize your inventory.

AVOID FIGHTING IN THE BEGINNING

If you are not wearing armor, do not jump straight away into fighting. You want to at least find some sort of protection first. If possible, sneak behind armored teammates on the front lines or just run away from fighting until you've found armor.

SQUAD ELIMINATED

PLACED #2 OF 20   7 SQUAD KILLS

MegaLuxx	ShellWarrior255	tatertot99420
KILLS 1	**KILLS** 0	**KILLS** 6
DAMAGE DEALT 618	**DAMAGE DEALT** 0	**DAMAGE DEALT** 1123
SURVIVAL TIME 17M 30S	**SURVIVAL TIME** 8M 27S	**SURVIVAL TIME** 17M 52S
PLAYERS REVIVED 0	**PLAYERS REVIVED** 0	**PLAYERS REVIVED** 2
PLAYERS RESPAWNED 0	**PLAYERS RESPAWNED** 0	**PLAYERS RESPAWNED** 0

KNOW YOUR WEAPONS

There are a lot of cool weapons in Apex, and many are pretty easy to use. But like any good weapon, they are also difficult to master. Learn how to use your weapon and even experiment with its modes and capabilities before you really need it under fire during combat.

STOP A FINISHER

You can actually stop someone from finishing a teammate if you catch them in the act. All you have to do is shoot at them, or even just punch them. Getting their attention off of the finishing move can stop it. But with finishing moves only lasting about 2-3 seconds, you have a very short window to halt it.

KILL A CHAMPION IN THE GAME, GET MORE POINTS

At the beginning of the game you see a lot of the info on display, such as showing you who the champion of the game is. This is who you want to target and take down for additional 500 XP and faster leveling.

CHAMPION SQUAD

500 XP
CHAMPION SLAYER BONUS

KNOW MORE ABOUT EACH OF YOUR MATCHES

You're paired with two other players, three in total. There are a total of 60 people playing the game at once, 20 teams in all. The games last between 14 and 25 minutes usually, which is lower than other similar games. The maps are also a bit more compact, which also helps make things go quicker.

The more you play Apex Legends, the better your muscle memory will become at performing the best fighting moves, the best finishing moves, and will even allow you to find new ways to get the most out of teamwork.

Everyone loves having hints and tricks to help them move higher up the skill ladder, but it is the practice, practice, practice of these tips and tactics that will make you a Legendary player!

YOU CAN ACTUALLY WALL CLIMB

You can't triple jump or run across the wall, but you can climb up it, giving you a different and interesting vantage point. You can climb up to 3x or 4x the height of your character when you sprint up a wall.

**You can also use doors to help you climb even higher than the wall or any other items you're climbing even higher.

FEATS AND FACTS

A brand-new game from Electronic Arts, Apex Legends has exploded in popularity since its launch in early 2019. With massive popularity comes intense interest, so we have compiled some fun facts and stats about the latest and greatest game in the popular battle royale genre.

- A mashup of a battle royale game and a hero-shooter, Apex brings all the compelling elements of the genres together in fresh way and opens up new challenges and goals.

- While there are limited animated shorts that go along with this game, EA also created backstories and biographies for the characters so you can familiarize yourself with them in different ways before playing with them.

- There are more than 60 million players playing Apex.

- Bloodhound was actually a character that was originally designed to be on Titanfall but landed on Apex.

- Apex Legends is FREE to play, but to get the most out of the game you should purchase certain extras, skins, packs, and the Battle Pass.

- You can choose from all of the characters that the game offers, you don't have to deal with getting a random one when you start the game.

- You cannot play as couples or even on your own in the game yet. You must play in teams of three.

- You don't have to wait for your team members to come around to revive you. You can actually revive yourself with the right items and time.

Shoot the plushes in this order:
1. Left of the Cascades
2. Skull Town
3. Slum Lakes
4. Left of Relay
5. Water Treatment Center
6. Right of Runoff
7. Right of Wetlands
8. Right of Hydro Dam
9. Bottom of Bunks
10. Right of Camps Next to the Water

- Apex has built in a pretty great anti-cheat feature to minimize that problem. They take cheating very seriously and have actually banned several hundred thousand cheaters.

- Nessie is the monster that you can find in odd places throughout the map. It will respawn at a new location every time. It is a little dino and she is just as cute as can be. Can you find her? If you want to see what she looks like, then go to the training or tutorial part of the game to locate her.

- If you shoot these smaller Nessies in a row then you might just be able to unlock a giant, actual version of her in the game. She emerges from the water in the last location that you shot the plush in.

- Lastimosa Armory is actually a character that can be found in Titanfall 2. He's the main captain and his name is found stamped on a few different weapons throughout.

- A lead designer hid a plush of his beloved dog in the South West portion of the training and tutorial map. You will need to climb a bit to get to him, but this little black friend might be worth it.

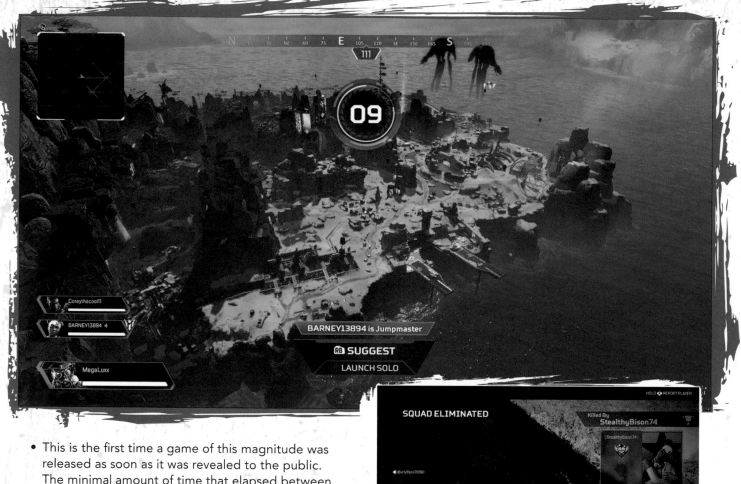

- This is the first time a game of this magnitude was released as soon as it was revealed to the public. The minimal amount of time that elapsed between the announcement and when people could play the game was exceptional.

- Developed by Respawn Entertainment and published by Electronic Arts.

- The game isn't really built for those that like to take others out through long-ranged weapons and battle, but rather for more close quarters combat.

- Punches lock the enemies in combat, though kicking is faster to get them down and keep them down if you're fighting without a weapon.

- Headshots, though beneficial and effective, are hard to do accurately.

- It is best to NEVER stay still because this is how others may be able to pick you off when they see you.

- You cannot hear your footsteps in Apex Legends, so if you think you could hear someone sneak up on you, think again.

- You can climb up on walls and buildings easily, making this a great way to get into new places and seize an advantage over those around you.

- When an enemy shield shatters, this gives off a very distinct sound.

- If you find the Ultimate Accelerants inside the game, which is a pretty big deal, then make sure to give it to the Lifeline class in the group. This is the best use of this feature in the game.

- There is a supply ship that is in the air that you can easily land on when you see it. You have to drop in this area to land on it though, and it might just move.

- It was rumored that pro gamer Ninja was paid $1 million to stream Apex Legends when it came out for the first time on his Twitch channel.

- There is a jumpmaster that is chosen at the beginning of the match. This is usually the third player and they choose where the people of the group land when they are in the air and about to jump into battle.

There are so many other hidden items and cool surprises you can find throughout the game. While the pace is fast and frantic, it is also pretty fun to discover all the Easter eggs developers have tucked into the game!

- More than 25 million gamers downloaded and played Apex within its first week of launch.

- 200+ million finishers have been used in Apex Legends since launch.

- 30% of players that play Apex Legends are new to EA games, and Apex is the first one they have played from this company.

CHAMPION SQUAD

🔊 BurlyBasil78981

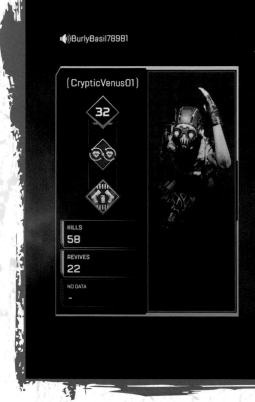

(CrypticVenus01)

32

KILLS
58

REVIVES
22

NO DATA
-

Top ranked in
last match

(BadApexer69)

13

KILLS
35

NO DATA
-

NO DATA
-

(KyleTheSavge)

18

KILLS
0

NO DATA
-

NO DATA
-

500 XP
CHAMPION SLAYER BONUS

APEX LEGENDS FREEBIES AND FUN!

If you're someone that loves spending time on Apex, and you want to cash in on some extras then you have come to the right place.

You can cash in on these extras, freebies, and fun that are being handed out for those players that love a good time while they are trying to make it to the top. Remember, teamwork is everything in Apex!

SUBSCRIBE TO GET FREEBIES

If you want some free loot and extras, you just have to sign up and subscribe to Origin Access, Xbox Exclusive EA Access, or PlayStation Plus.

EA NEWSLETTER

When you sign up for the EA newsletter through their website, you can also take advantage of some freebies and stay in the loop for when new ones are handed out.

SOCIAL MEDIA

Follow Apex Legends on Instagram, Twitter, and YouTube to get more exclusive content, bonus offers, and freebies from the developers.

LEVEL-UP YOUR ACCOUNT

You can add free skins and extras to your account when you level up. Even if you do not have the Battle Pass, you can still get extras that come from being able to get a higher leveled player.

COLLECT & USE CRAFTING METALS

It might take a bit of time, but the more crafting metals you have, the more you're able to get quality skins from them. It is known as crafting, but you're essentially buying the skins with the metal that you have.

HAVE TWITCH PRIME?

If you have a Twitch Prime account then you can link your Twitch account to the EA account that you need to play the game, and this will welcome and open up Apex packs and a Pathfinder skin that is given to you for free.

You can also get Twitch Prime rewards for free when you have these accounts linked to one another.

As the Apex Legends world keeps evolving and expanding, the best way to gain more knowledge about it is to keep playing it. Play hard, have fun, and find out if you have what it takes to be a Legend!

CONCLUSION

For those who are searching for an action-packed battle royale game to play with more customization than ever before, you have come to the right place. Apex Legends is the state of the art in this very large genre.

With gamers from all over the world signing on, you never know who you are going to get paired up with. But no matter where they are or where you are, you must come together as a team and understand that your collective strength is greater than your individual parts. Those that grasp that first, will be best.

Everyone has the same common goal to win, so it is up to you and your teammates to determine if you are going to engage in the type of give-and-take that you see from the best teams, and become Legends yourselves!

Agent Florida01

NOW SELECTING

2

◀) BLA

WAITIN

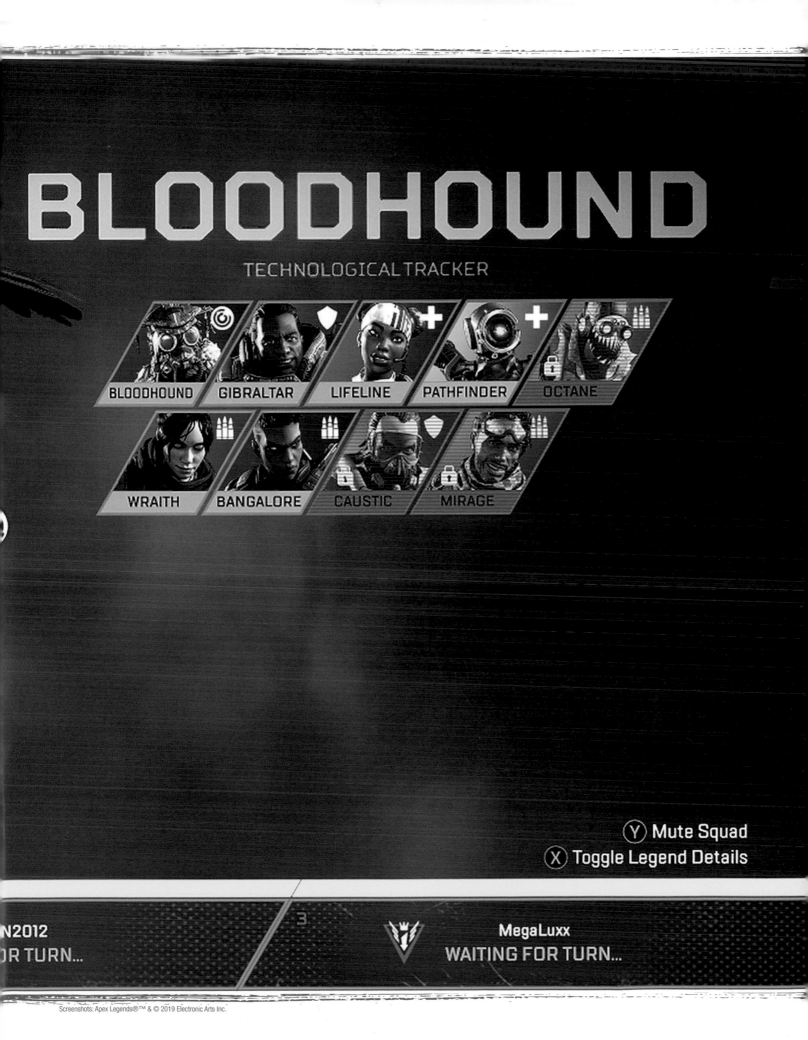

BLOODHOUND

TECHNOLOGICAL TRACKER

BLOODHOUND   GIBRALTAR   LIFELINE   PATHFINDER   OCTANE

WRAITH   BANGALORE   CAUSTIC   MIRAGE

(Y) Mute Squad
(X) Toggle Legend Details

N2012   3   MegaLuxx
OR TURN...   WAITING FOR TURN...